Light Sources

Throughout his career, **Charles Seliger** (American, 1926–2009) pursued an inner world of organic abstraction, celebrating the structural complexities of natural forms. Inspired by a wide range of literature in natural history, biology, and physics, he cultivated a poetic style of abstraction that explored the dynamics of order and chaos animating the celestial, geographical, and biological realms. Seliger paid homage to nature's infinite variety and his paintings have been described as "microscopic views of the natural world".

Born in New York City but raised in Jersey City, Seliger never completed high school or received formal art training. In 1943, he befriended artist Jimmy Ernst and was quickly drawn into the circle of avant-garde artists championed by Howard Putzel and Peggy Guggenheim. Two years later, at the age of nineteen, Seliger was included in the groundbreaking 67 Gallery exhibition *A Problem for Critics*, and had his first solo show at Guggenheim's Art of This Century gallery. At the time, Seliger was the youngest artist exhibiting with members of the abstract expressionist movement, and he was only twenty years old when the Museum of Modern Art acquired his painting *Natural History: Form within Rock* (1946). In 1950, Seliger obtained representation from Willard Gallery, forming close friendships with artists Mark Tobey, Lyonel Feininger, and Norman Lewis. By 1949, Seliger had his first major museum exhibition at the de Young Memorial Museum, San Francisco. During his lifetime, his art was celebrated in over forty-five solo shows at prominent galleries in New York and Europe. In 1986, Seliger was given his first retrospective at the Solomon R. Guggenheim Museum, which now holds the largest collection of his work. His work is also represented in numerous public institutions including the Metropolitan Museum of Art, the Museum of Modern Art, and the Whitney Museum of American Art. In 2003, Seliger received the Pollock-Krasner Foundation's Lee Krasner Award in recognition of his long and illustrious career in the arts. In 2005, the Morgan Library and Museum acquired his journals – 148 hand-written volumes produced between 1952 to 2009. In 2012, the Mint Museum in Charlotte, North Carolina organized the traveling exhibition *Seeing the World Within: Charles Seliger in the 1940s*.

Light Sources

Poems

DAVID JAFFIN

First published in the United Kingdom in 2013 by
Shearsman Books
50 Westons Hill Drive
Emersons Green
Bristol BS16 7DF

Shearsman Books Ltd Registered Office
30–31 St. James Place, Mangotsfield, Bristol BS16 9JB
(this address not for correspondence)

www.shearsman.com

ISBN 978-1-84861-302-7

Distributed for Shearsman Books in the U. S. A.
by Small Press Distribution, 1341 Seventh Avenue, Berkeley, CA 94710
E-Mail orders@spdbooks.org
www.spdbooks.org

Production, composition & cover design: Edition Wortschatz, a service of
Neufeld Verlag, Schwarzenfeld/Germany
E-Mail info@edition-wortschatz.de, www.edition-wortschatz.de

Title picture:
Charles Seliger (1926–2009)
Monoliths (detail), 1995
acrylic on Masonite
12 1/2″ x 10″, signed and dated
Courtesy of Michael Rosenfield Gallery, LLC, New York, NY
www.michaelrosenfeldart.com

Printed in Germany

Contents

7

13

Thanks to
Marina Moisel
for her continued help
with these poetic manuscripts

*I've been often asked why I break words
between lines. As Lenore, one of my most
perceptive readers said, "You don't really break
words between lines, but place them within
the entire rhythmic flow of the poem.*

*As my poems are extremely condensed I don't
want words, especially the longer ones, to be
"hanging out", therefore this very musical need
for such a continuing on. Word–break, if one
wants to call it that, means that these words
must be put back together again, almost as if
they've become recreated, newly realized.*

David Jaffin

Seeing-him-through

She looked

as if she
was trying

to see-him-
through

with eyes
that could

only hold
their surfac

ing mean
ings.

Repeat

ing theme

s and sense-
symboliz

ing what's
continuous

ly more than
a single

light-glan
ce.

Early-morn

ing bells

brighten
ing in the con

suming dark
ness of all

these indwell
ing fear

s.

Some hurts

can bleed
so intense

ly–deep
that little'

s left of
one's own

self–inscrib
ing blood–cur

rents.

Airport terminal poems (3)

a) Time decide

s here mot
ionless spa

ces length
ening an ex

panse of
endless

ly waiting.

b) Winter

lights dim

ly sound
ing these

wind–surr
ounding si

lences.

c) Window

ed glass

as sound
lessly ap

parent as
those distant

flights of
time–ascend

ing bird
s.

Viola Concerto *(K. Stamitz, last mvt.)*

catchy tune

that catch
es us off–

balancing
the where of

not being
there for

long.

Omaha Beach 1944

Fire–sand

cold–steel–
touch runn

ing the death
route through

those blood–
streaming

s out.

A little

lone black
lady (only

one on the
plane) agèd–

beyond–her–
years narrow

ing-down look
sadly self-in

habiting.

Tiled floor

s always

left him
hard-down

space-con
scious of

each step'
s time-re

newing.

City of

lights glass–

intent puls
ing the dark

with their
artificial

self-search
ings.

The shallow'

s blue heron

image deepen
ing an ap

pearance
of depthed-

solitude
s.

Drive-in

motels nei

ther-coming-
nor-going

but always
s one-of-the-

other's rest
lessly unfind

ing.

Kaleb

if there'

s ever-left
a kind of

sweetness
in a man

not effem
inate but of

even-temper
ed smooth-

sailing
s.

A penny-a-

poem evalu

ating those
higher-held

values of a
money-orien

ted bright
ly-minted

society.

Where Gauguin'

s dense-color

ings a way
of reattun

ing himself
to those prim

eval darkness
es deeply

within.

Rock-foun

    tain's flow

    ing light-
    source

    d a cool
    ness of un

    touched ap
    pearance

    s.

Diminished

    In the sha

    dowing reach
    of tall buil

    dings he felt
    himself di

    minished to
    a lesser

    sense of
    self-being.

Snake

    in the brush

    wood's ground-
    rhythmic a

    wareness
    es.

My father

once so in

securely
shy came out

of himself
the way a

snake cast
s its out–

used skin a
side.

H. H.

When the

pains became
unbearab

ly intense
He gave up

on–life did
n't recipro

cate in like–
manner.

Low tide'

s surfaced–

quietude
s as if the

sea had be
come tamed

to its voice
less presen

ce.

Women

may dress

their own
sense-for-be

ing as a doll
they were

once clothed
with their

own person
ally colored

intention
s.

Can we

learn to

feel what we'
ve never known

before as the
death of a

dying friend
in the clear

blue of all
this Floridi

an bright
ness.

Dialogued

This stone

only become
s alive

through the
warmth-cool

ness of his
awareness

es'-touch.

For Rosemarie

swam her

self through
the bodied

coolness
of her re

freshing re
newal.

Chang

ing train

s in the
midst of a

one-track
approach

ing those un
known station

s of time'
s increasing

ly self-inhab
iting full

ness.

Defeated

powers as the

American South
live on through

the ever-re
curring nost

algia of
those alway

s lost-time
s.

Low tide'

s mild wave

s calming
those wind–

stilled mo
ment's light–

increasing.

Here

at Ft. Myer'

s Edison re
sort–home

celebrat
ing Christ

mas with arti
ficial light

s as if the
discover

er was being
honored and

not the bright
ness of that

real–guiding
star birth

ed in the
true light

of the God–
given child.

Some of

that "tongue-

in-cheek" less
provoking hu

mour pucker
ed Pink to

the very-lip
s of his al

ways bright
ly sanctifi

ed New Year'
s resolut

ions.

H. H.

After year

s of practis
ing from all-

sides most e
very organ

Death gave-up-
on-him left

hovering
for life un

til he let
be cut-off

that last
link holding

him fastly-
here.

The eternal swimmer

He swam back

and forth
and back hour

s-on-end
until that

pool lifed
the measure

of his very-
being.

A final leave

We took a

final leave
(hesitant

ly at first)
from all we'

d ever-known
of his death-

becoming i
mage.

Pelican

s soundless

ly gliding
through the

wind-spaced
currents of

dreamed-a
wakening

s.

A "meeting-

of-the-mind
s" or the

lips or of
touched-re

vealing
those (as

yet) unchar
tered person

al landscap
ings.

Window

ed transpar

ently light-
focusing

those most
ly interior

dark–place
s.

Primeval

swamp–land

s snake–con
cealing that

most intimate
ly poison

ous fear–
sense.

He decided

for death'

s no–return
route but

each day be
came the more

life–of–him
as if that

nearness
to death in

creasing
his life–call

ings.

Dementia

Her sense–

for-being
vaguely mut

ed her in
creasing

ly loss-from-
self.

She gave

him that dead–

eyed fish–
stare as if

she'd been
pulled from

the sandied
depth of her

fully sleep
ful contemplat

ions.

Alice

The wrong

side of self
.married the

wrong man at
the worst

possible
time that her

better-self
(which only e

merged then)
paying for

long-timed
loneliness.

For Lenore

Does your

room of his
pictures

sleep at
night or are

their eye
s awake to

whatever
dreams have

flowed
through your

interior
darkness

es.

Climbing

> hills over-
>
> looking the
> town's histor
>
> ic past now
> nakedly embra
>
> cing its cold
> take-down ap
>
> pearance.

Bared-empt

> ied woods
>
> self-denying
> the leaf-spread
>
> of its soft
> ly known life-
>
> rhythms.

Murmuring *(Charles Seliger 1986)*

> so perfect
>
> ly conciev
> ed as if
>
> color had be
> come so sound
>
> lessly awake.

She heard

so little

that the
world seem

ed as a
dream ines

capably
past.

American

flags fast–

flying the
wounded

ness of their
blood–red

coloring
s.

Night–

lights wind–

searching
the unspoken

realms of
distanc

ing star
s.

Wendy

Her love he

felt had
turned cold

despite the
subtle warm

th of her
less–intend

ing smile.

The young

est child
always thor

oughly pro
tected until

they all died–
off and left

her helpless
ly disarmed.

Even those

most deep

ly spaced
slow-movement

s can't slow–
down the sur

facing place
of life's ir

resistible
no-holding

s-back.

Smoke invis

ibly releas

ed as if a
scending

prayers to
those unseen

all-encompass
ing blued-

realms.

"Automatic

writing" ap

pears like
that Christ-

icon "not
painted by

human hand"
mystical

ly self-ap
parent.

Those na

ked woods

stripped
of their ap

parent green
to the soul-

source of
emptied phras

ings.

Gentile Fab

riano's lyri

cal abundance
phrasing the

rhythmic
source of

their self-
describing

coloring
s.

This stone'

s numbed-mut

ed sounds
lasting

out their
prolong

ing length-
for-touch.

Scarsdale'

s a mirror

ing town of
vacant win

dows enclos
ing imitat

ion pre-revol
utionary

made-up ap
pearance

s.

Hemingway'

s muscle-

bound manli
ness left a

finely–deep
er sensibil

ity not e
ven for wo

men he'd only
marry with a

500 pound mar
lin brought–

in boat-side.

January 16 *(4)*

a) the family en

circled him
(the dying)

with phases of
his life's

dream as if
there was no

other way
out to dis

tant calling
s they kept

him now close
ly-theirs.

b) They kept

touching

that moment–
of–no–return

as if his
dead–hand'

s still life–
absorbing.

c) We both ob

servors and
friends out

side and yet
drawn–in

to those self–
revealing

family death–
bonds.

d) Morning-

after bright

and still as
usual as if

time had
only left him

and that close
ly formed mourn

ing behind.

Sand-flower

s clasping

for light
rooted in

the living
source of

a dead–down
dryness.

Helmut

(U. S. A. renam

ed Leroy)
land and time

divided
as if two–

personed
facing both

ways–out.

Night-wave

s darkly ap

parent as if
a dreamed

continui
ty of moon-
like tidal

expressive
ness.

Little girl

hand-hold

ing right up
to the very-

height of her
father's

protective
shadowing

s.

Low-tide'

s soft and

quieting
wind's sur

facing the
reach of its

vastly un
touchable

expanse
s.

I only

knew he had

died when
he wasn't

there any
more Death

realizes
a place of

missing per
sons but not

the moment
of his actual

decease.

As he said

"I always
got what I

wanted" e
ven death

needed to a
wait his

final call
ings.

Too sweet

she appear

ed (as most
English dessert

s) to harden
to the pain–

stricken
confines of

Christ's
nailed and

dried-down
body.

A lone sea

gull sitting

on an aband
oned pole

staring out
distance

s of his un
reclaiming

thereness.

A pastel

light-sens

ing prett
ily-smiling

skied the
day he was

lowered in
to the last

confines of
earth's cold

ly-moist en
closure

s.

These soft

waves so

gently cover
ing over e

ven those
most-last

ing pains-
of-loss.

Are these

stuffed wild
animals

children
so caress

ingly adore
protect

ing them
selves a

gainst their
own not-so-

expressive
ly-nice ani

mal instinct
s.

She used all

the resource
es at her

command
tempting lip

s sensuous
ly infold

ing hair and
those come-

on eyes that
held him

short of
crossing

that no-re
turn line.

The "real parents"

Who were "the
real parent

s" Those blood-
related

denying a
common life

together
Or those blood

lessly lifed
to another

sense-for-be
ing.

Was Monet

the first to

realize the
transpar

encies of
light-color

ings Or did
his brush

paint him to
reveal its o

therwise
ness.

For Rosemarie

voiced in an

inner silence
of express

ive togeth
erness.

Pieter de

Hooch "a dom

estic painter"
when that

very-room's
space-open

ing light-re
vealing.

The sound

of these

waves reced
ing into

those unspok
en silence

s of near–
remember

ed thought
s.

He "wasn'

t himself"
he said Who

was that self
in the night

called to an
estranged

sense–of–
place dark

ly self–in
habiting.

Sourced

Searching

for the source
of a rare dis

ease neither
named nor da

ted began
secretly to

inhabit
them.

Sleeping-walk

ing Lady Macbeth

discover
ed that invis

ible blood in
vading her

own couldn'
t be rubbed

or even dream
ed-off.

Off-side

jumping

the gun the
race became

his own circ
ling the

lone routes
of that empt

ied track.

3 sisters (3)

a) Michelle'

s down-to-
earth way of

standing her
time's self-

determin
ing cool.

b) Alice'

s warmth-in
volving o

ver-flow.

c) Julie a

little-girl-

lost her mo
ther's fairy-

tale-like.

Horse shoe'

s iron-dull

ed ringing
sounds soft

ly escounc
ed in the

quiet sand
s of their

all–impend
ing circu

lar touch.

A game-soc

iety as if

the "real
life" contin

uously shad
owing its

child–like
off-spring

s.

Reading him

self backward

s until he
realized

that time it
self a two–

way street
in alternat

ing direct
ions.

Norman

faithed-in

the name of
an unknown

god facing
the near-com

ing claims
of an imper

sonal death.

If a funer

al's a "feast-

of-life" then
a christen

ing's a birth
ed-death be

ginnings and
end a unity-

of-the-same.

She became

so used to ar

tificial flow
ers that when

real one's
feel of

their tender–
softness re

vealed a new
and strange

sense–for–color
ings.

Roomed

Old and a

lone in time
she became

roomed with
those phant

om images of
lost memor

ies.

Puzzled

He became

so intricate
ly involved

in puzzles
that his

"real life"
didn't quite

fit–back to
its preaccust

omed place.

Poem

s that don'

t write-them
selves-out

resemble per
sons too clothe-

conscious
ly self-de

ceiving.

At the shuff

le-board her
competit

ive face-lip
s tensely

reaching-out
eyes scann

ing self-suff
iciently.

Her kite

as it seem

ed almost
cloud-reveal

ing motion
lessly time-

escaping.

Joseph Roth *(1894–1939)*

Only the class

ical clarity
of his time-

subduing pen
kept him a

lert to a
world sink

ing deeply
within the

sadnesses
of his drink-

consuming
person.

Florida'

s swamp-land

s once reclus
ively-prime

val now drain
ed-down from

the myth of
their haunted

Indian past.

Snake

s lurking pois

onously alive
through the

unkept brush-
grasses of

their moon
ed dream–like

appearan
ces.

Are lang

uages voiced

so deeply with
in our very–

being pre–hist
orically ori

gined from
their all–per

suasive land–
scaping

s.

Too shy

to realize

the pretty
patterns of

her modest
ly self-be

coming dress.

Sanderling'

s feet-find
ing scarce

ly sound-re
viving a

commonly in
creasing

route.

Shell-seek

er's small-in

timate touch
finger

ing sound-sen
sings.

Their house

darkly inhabi

ted with sus
picious ru

mours whis
pering scarce

ly aloud.

Flower

s blooming

the invisible
dark's un

touched si
lences.

Lime disease

invisibly

haunting the
outer reach

es of his
bodied blood

fullness.

First meet

ing's feeling

each other
out that

vague dual
ity of me-

and-there.

Genesis 19

If Lot offer

ed his two
"untouched"

daughter
s to Sodom'

s sex-crav
ing mob per

haps redeem
ing his pre

angelic soul
How much ear

thy sinful
ness will The

Lord tolerate
our "not-

looking-back".

For Rosemarie

It's that

very feminine-
softness of

your through-
reaching

timeless
claims-on-

me.

Choice-of-gifts

How few of

us realize
that Salomon

ian choice-
of-gifts The

real choice is
His not our

s pre-timed
to the source

of our very-
being.

The funeral

that Goethe

never attend
ed of his wife

mother best
friend out of

fear of a
higher claim-

on-life more
than his-own?

High-borne

shadows dis

tantly cross
ing the beach

es' silent in
tonation

s.

Reflect

ing flower

ed impress
ions indis

tinctly
glassed.

Whisper

ed inreveal

ing word'
s wind-phras

ings.

Dead-end

stopped him

right–there
stone–entran

ced.

Butter

flies illu

minating
their waver

ing unbalan
cing flight–

designs.

An island

of birds

self-surround
ing their

shadow
ing flight–

instinct
s.

Some can

even feel

the less–ap
parent weight

of their
sound–embrac

ing shadow
s.

Parasail

Sky-deep

those umbrel
laed hands

of his hold
ing-fast to

a space
less blue.

Mood mo

> ments over
>
> shadowing
> Pink's deli
>
> ciously
> smiled ice–
>
> creaming
> s.

The gull

> flying its
>
> sound–escap
> ing shadow
>
> lightward
> s.

Her violin

> stringed to
>
> those sustain
> ing inner ac
>
> cords of
> self-reveal
>
> ing hand-
> sense.

He eyed

her awake

with that
shadowing

sense of
dreamed–en

closure
s.

"He left his

mark" where

to whom and
at what cost

those flesh–
wounds daily

scarred from
their previous

blood–re
lease.

Boredom'

    s a state-of–

    mind encompas
    sing more of

    him that e
    ven time

    could success
    fully concede.

When the

    slender palm
    's graceful

    ly time-reach
    ing the length

    of its long–
    withhold

    ing lyrical
    phrasing

    s.

His chair

    now vacant

    ly inhabit
    ing its death–

    fulfilling
    silence

    s.

When

color be

comes espec
ially appar

ent while
dark–conceal

ing.

It "speak

s for itself"

when the see
ing's so a

livened word
lessly word–

creating.

The theme

s may re

peat them
selves But

the words re
define their

intricate
ly other–

sensed see
ings.

Taking side

s for a final

show–down he
preferred

the side–
lines as the

game increas
ingly lifed

itself out.

If-clause *(for Warren)*

s without a re

solution be
cause there

aren't any ex
cept the o

pening length
of the quest

ioning self.

Looking

down at what'

s looking up
with that slight

ly insinuat
ing sense-of–

superior
ity.

Cloth-patt

erns sensed–

for-touch
ing through

their prede
termining

express
ive color

ings.

Paled

> This morn
>
> ing's fad
> ing moon pal
>
> ed those sand
> s with its
>
> lesser–con
> cealing after
>
> touch.

We realized

> only the lim
>
> ited reach of
> a bird's fra
>
> gile–single
> claw and its
>
> self–surround
> ing blood–i
>
> maged remain
> s.

Those senti

> mental Hollywood
>
> tear–jerker
> s leave me
>
> only with
> this dry–i

ronic need
for a convinc

ing self-de
fense.

Open-ending

s (as those

favored by
Chekhov) leave

the reader con
tinuously

closing-in
for that much-

needed addit
ional proof.

Sail

boats horizon

ed to the out
er-rim of her

self-expos
ing surfac

ing thought
s.

Moods

are like the

ever-chang
ing depths-of-

clouds they
darken or dis

perse leav
ing us alone

irreversib
ly time-sitt

ing.

It begin

s before our

knowing the-
why-or-where

as sudden as
those first

spring flow
ers fresh

ly colored-
for-life.

3 Modern ways *(3)*

a) *Abbreviations*

A world of

the insider'
s specially

adorned abbrev
iations left

this outsider
dumb-found

ed.

b) *Statistic*

s so impress

ively assem
bled left him

alone in a
forest of un

identifi
able being

s.

c) Talk show

s those wash

ed–and–dried–
down thought–

clothes hang
ing out their

contrary o
pinions

until they'
ve been talk

ed–out of
all their re

maining col
ors.

So unimagin

ably fat he

sat on an out
spreading full

ness of wood–
choking dis

play.

"My foolish heart"

the tone and

word–sense
perfectly

balancing
a truth that

consumed much
of her very-

being.

Low

tides calmed

to the smooth
ed surface

s of their
slowly re

ceding shore
d-calling

s.

Chameleons *(for M. S.)*

Are the chang

ing-color
chameleon

s an uncon
scious sign of

our merg
ing into a

world still
foreign to

our own.

An imprison

ed pelican

blood-flesh
ed hooked to

the holding-
depth of its

unimagined
pain-source.

The language

the birds

sing (however
brightly sub

duing) seem
s inescap

ably self-real
izing.

The beach'

s ice-cream-

man seemed al
most at his

breath's end
pushing his

sun-heavy
cart for the

pleasurable
eyes of

young fresh-
ly-looking con

sumers.

Aged-out

Nothing

left for him
to do Aged-

out retired
to those lone

ly spells of
compelling

silence.

When his

world became

but a pale
image of his

own time-re
ceding per

son.

Our pleasure

boat's slow

ed down to
the speed of

those self-ex
posing inter

ior sound-
views.

Under

bridged

hollowed
self-enclos

ing sound'
s time-reach

ing.

For Rosemarie

Your hand

pulsing my
mind's flow

as the ri
ver's cease

lessly quiet
ing course.

Genuinely so!

It's that

living-out
of those oft–

unrealized
self–contra

diction
s that fash

ion us genu
inely so!

A voice

newly worded

is like a dress
accenting

unreveal
ed phrased–

response
s.

Poor Miss Bart

let grammar
ed to a less

resilent
sense-for-life

lessly stone–
imaged.

Beach

walkers

at the dawn
of their scar

cely touch
ed wind-a

wakenings.

He slept

through

the increas
ing dark of

dreamed-si
lences.

These grace

ful hill-
sloping apoll

onic dolphin
s shadow

lessly time-
recalling.

Lithe-

little liz
ards self-e

longating
thinly ex

posing sun-
lit solitu

des.

She was

like an un

flagged ship
set loose

harbor
ing remote

sea-drift
ings.

This night

receding

as the tide'
s breathed-

in moon-be
spoken.

Danger-

signals red–

flashing re
curring eye–

sensing a
larms.

Mild Flori

dian warmth

reminding
of my mother'

s protecting
smiles clos

ing me in
bed–tight

to my own i
magining

moon–full
nesses.

Pelican

sound–glid

ing the wave'
s outlast

ing wind–
phrasing

s.

Butter

flies nervous

ly dance-ex
pressing

their off-
beat color

ings.

Hearing

the rain'

s slow-down
to a world

of interior-
felt intim

acies.

Titian

landscap

ed the inner
coloring

s of his
thought-

felt mytholo
gical scene

s.

Low-tide

the sea voice
lessly sooth

ing out its con
templative

quietude
s.

Flora *(Titian)*

the goddess
of spring en

ticing the
flower-re

vealing
touch of her

own beauti
fying presen

ce.

Crown of Thorns *(Titian)*

The stone-cool

ness of the Em
peror's tower

ing glanc
ed Jesus into

a helpless
ly imitating

submission.

For Rosemarie

complete

s her voice
less presence

enclosing all
that I couldn'

t have known
of my vastly

interior
self.

Swelling *(in memory E. W.)*

passions
high-tided

him away
from all those

domestic
boundar

ies that had
marked out his

flourishing
fully-estab

lished age-
lengths.

Artificial

flower's

dried shad
ows vased to

a depth of
waterless

light.

Bicycling

the beach

wheeling up
right thought'

s steadied
hand–hold.

Zail

boats indis

tinctly hori
zoned drift

ing out the
currents of

their unre
membered ti

dal awaken
ings.

Shakespeare'

s sonnets so

richly color
ing a depth

ed–fullness
of their al

ways express
ive here–for–

now.

Are Titian'

s portrait

s mirror
ing the sub

ject's own
sense of self–

revealing
Or are they fresh

ly seen inclus
ively realiz

ing the only-
now.

A dull-

timed dried

sand–down
day inexpress

ively non–com
pliant.

She try

ing to mea

sure his step
to her own

life–long
keeping–up–

with.

Phil

He left me

with a left–
out look

sheepish
ly hiding

from his u
sual strong–

man self–e
vident appear

ance.

For Matthew

He had to

say–it–all
but once

said it still–
seemed unfin

ished as if
words couldn'

t quite satis
fy their vague

ly less–encom
passing sense

d–meaning
s.

These root-

    entangled
    southern–wood

    ed forests
    left him with

    a need for un
    ravelling

    his own self–
    contradict

    ing time–phas
    ings.

Flat

    sands stretch

    ing his thought
    s out to an

    equal sense
    of timed–be

    ing.

Her u

sually self–

smiling face
concealing

phases of un
touched inner

silence
s.

Jesus

storied his

timeless
truths as

those high–
mountain

passes into
dialogue

s of unanswer
able respon

se.

A cat's

eyes slowly o

pening the re
ceding dark

nesses of its
predator'

s claw–tast
ing–for–gain.

Arcadia

Florida

once a thriv
ing cattle–

town tracked to
the deadly

end–station
of their blood–

meated calling
s.

These si

lent sandy

shores time
lessly receiv

ing as the
eternal woman'

s softly touch
ing wave's car

essing sound-
flow.

A bald woman

denied of

her inner-
reaching beau

tifying hair-
flow must

feel as naked
ly assessed

as the Eve of
ancient bibli

cal times.

Open-end

ings of the

kind that
leave us

high-hold
ing unresolv

ed see-saw
s.

Aging

    men rarely a

    vailing of
    that self-se

    curing wis
    dom looking

    more like
    caged-in

    animals too
    long phased-

    out domesti
    cating.

For Pete

    that little
    dog ear-a

    wake eager
    to see what

    he couldn'
    t understand

    time-endear
    ing its mo

    mentary
    watch.

Arcadia

Florida

blood-haunt
ing these pre-

Auschwitz
cattle-train

s tracked to
their dead-

ended route.

Taking

the measure
of his own

self-assur
ing stride

each step as
if pre-imag

ining thought-
touch.

These wave

> s slowly e
>
> ven softly
> envelop
>
> ing a contin
> uity of
>
> time's self-
> evolving
>
> complete
> ness.

The creative mind *(for G. D.)*

> sleeps the
> growth of i
>
> deas form
> ing to their
>
> awakening
> brightness.

In this Flor

> idian winter
>
> even the in
> visible
>
> snakes cold-
> staring for
>
> the warmth of
> their blood-

intensing pois
onous aware

ness.

Tiny

birds inspir

ing these pale
sands with

their rapid–rhy
thmically

all–attending
feet.

A woman pour (Vermeer)

ing the milk–
suspending

stillness
es cooling

this room's
most certain

ly awared
coloring

s.

Night

     tides the

     moon voice
     lessly awaken

     ing the dark
     ening spirit'

     s undiscov
     ered deep.

Why did Ver

     meer's model
     s seldom eye–

     sense–us to
     a complet

     ion of their
     touched–near

     nesses.

Intricate

quilt–flow

er–design
s intimate

ly describ
ing the rest

less color
ings of his

all–envelop
ing sleep.

Night-tim

ed roses sha
dowlessly

touched to
their scent–de

scribing still
nesses.

Aging

coins as poem

s only in
crease the

value of
their rarify

ing design
if they display

few signs of
having been

worn–down
from use.

A bird

tensed–in

the close
winds follow

ing its
dark shadow'

s echo
ing flight.

A starless

night even

the winds in
distinct

ly phrasing
their inde

cipherable
cause.

My father'

s first fresh

ly-pressed o
range juice

after week
s of conval

escence tas
ted the new

ness of his
very-being.

Small

birds rapid

ly dotting
the beach with

their scarce
ly definable

touch-mark
s.

The stair

s slowly cur

ving step upon
the continu

ous phases of
life gather

ing shadow
s behind until

at ground–bott
om he silent

ly disappear
ed into a

vast world of
no–beyond

ness.

Abbreviat

ing words from

their unknown
source until

as artifi
cial flower

s they out
bloomed e

ven their
scent

less origin.

It's the

still‑spoken

Vermeer's
nothing but

light‑cool‑
coloring

s and the
touch‑feel of

soundless
ly enlighten

ing.

A thought

an image so
suddenly

there was a
falling star'

s reclaim
ing darkness.

The dash

between

birth and
death your

tombstone'
s final life-

enclosing
with even

less than a
word's time-

span.

The Indian

s here the

Jews there
hated to the

bone and now
buried in the

inordinate
praise of a

speech
less respon

se.

She was as

>fat as she
>
>was friend
>ly over
>
>flowing
>with short–
>
>eyed flesh
>ly smile
>
>s.

"Nothing'

>s new under
>
>the sun"
>unless it'
>
>s seen and
>worded to
>
>its unique
>refreshing
>
>thereness.

Low

>tide's when
>the sea with
>
>draws to its
>self-encom
>
>passing still
>nesses.

The snake

s the black

ones appear
ing at night

Their eye
s staring

the moon
less inhab

iting dark.

With the

apparent

ease–of–the–
dolphin Pink

ornamental
ly dressed in

the orange–
original

ly self–fully
expanding

his oncoming
swim–tide

s.

Realizing

He needed

that cold-
touch embrac

ing metallic-
sense to real

ize the blood-
depth of his

own person
al exposure

s.

So made-up

for her sixty
some years

that she could
n't even see

through to
her self-deny

ing past.

Some women

are so con

scious of be
ing looked

at that not
even 50 meter

s could se
parate them

from that
magnetic-

reach.

While two

men shadow–

standing
dog lies bet

ween the tempt
ing coolness

of the sand'
s envelop

ing softly es
caping dream

s.

This room

silent

ly window
ing the sea'

s distanc
ing darkness

es.

Children'

s eyes may

realize more
opening realm

s of undis
covered

though sound
less vista

s.

If man'

s the-mea-

sure-of-all
things then

let us not
forget the

feet and in
ches of his

depth-descend
ing coffin.

Those inno

cently appear

ing Bahamas'
blue holes

down the dang
erous caves

into the lost
depths of

those sunken
watering

deadly re
mains.

For C. F.

She inhabit
ed that blond-

devotional
look of a

hand-envelop
ing cherub

blue-eyed
heavenly as

piring for
ceremon

ial purpose
s.

No one'

s left with

out scars
the invisible

ones healing
less thor

oughly blood-
reaching the

secret source
of our most

privately pro
tected do

mains.

For Rosemarie'

s sweet kiss

es as the
scent of soft

rose petal
s touching

through the
very-depth

s of the sea'
s reclaim

ing shore–
times.

Snow-voic

ed sounding

the wind'
s outlast

ing timeless
ness.

Dark

snow the

night breath
ing a depth

of immaculate
ly arousing

star–birth
s.

Our child

ren may (at

times) be
felt blood–

close though
the imprint

s they leave
behind strange

ly dissimilar
from our own.

Street

lights re

claiming
mysterious–

glassed dark
nesses.

Karl Stamitz

s' wind be

spoken catch-
me–ups into

ever–remind
ing hearsay

s.

Melting

snow's un

covering a
world of

winter–froz
en silent

self–re
vealing

s.

Phantom

tree winter-
frozen its

timeless
need for self–

recalling.

Smoke

shadow

lessly wind-
drifting

express
ive silen

ces.

Snowman

inhabiting

a kingdom
of sound

less wind-
baring dis

tances.

My father'

s friend

less child
hood left

something
of the speech

less need of
that child-

in-him al
ways-there.

Each poem

as a hand-be

spoken snow
man inhabit

ing but a
transcient

sense of "al
ways-now".

When their

carefully–

packed snow
man started

melting their
distant child–

like death-i
magining

s.

A lone

ly diminish

ing voice
from those

lost-pre
vailing snow–

receding dis
tances.

Skating

the light re-

freshing
surfaces of

their indwell
ing down-be

low feared-
darkness

es.

Skiing

that opened-
aired free-

from-all
time-releas

ing.

The snow

melting its

serene-si
lences away

and left this
land naked

ly exposed.

Animalled

If boxing'

s (as they
say) the true

measure of
one's mascu

linity blood–
bruising-down

the opponent'
s sense-of–

being the
way animal

s instinct
ively lock–

horns appeal
ing for their

lady's spec
ializing

favour
s.

Competit

ive should

mostly-mean
matching–

up to the
very-best

of one's
own special

124

ly-preferr
ed self-patt

erns.

Beaten as

a child by

her war-home-
coming-father

she rare
ly return

ed to those
rooms still

screaming-out
echoing

pains and
fears.

If

you don't

standup to
bullies they'

ll stand-you
down their

ground-pro
truding

grimace
s.

My life'

s becoming
interwov

en with dream
s that leave

a tapestry
of a scarce

ly remember
ed past be

hind.

Pre-spring

the land

still heavy
with the weight

of winter'
s uneasing

depth as if
wombed in

an unseen
darkness

always there
life–sus

taining.

An "eye-opener"

They call it

an "eye-open
er" as if

we're witness
ing only half–

blind now
that disen

chanting
self.

It "dawned

on him" the

morning'
s increas

ingly light–
being as if

self-reali
zing.

Nielsen'

s Clarinet

Concerto
so personal

izing the
performer

he knew that
the instru

ment itself
robbed of

its other
wise flow

ing-lyrical
nature.

"Give and take"'s

a two-handed
method of

balancing
one's sit-

down compo
sure.

Snow

drops appear
ing as inno
cent after

thought
s or as the

French say
"pierced-

snow"'s ex
tending

blade.

At the birth

of spring e
ven as the

snow melt
s a kind

of soft-
sadness in

the air
yet still

vaguely a
live.

Even at 74

the spring'

s unquiet
ing more of

my being
thawed–down

the inner
depths of

these sap
less longing

s.

Violin Concerto no. 1 (Mozart)

I only knew

and felt it
was Mozart

with the slow
movement'

s so easing
harmonic

climbs the
freshness

of its first–
spring's re

calling.

The Mendels

sohn of the
Athalia Over

ture is one
I could e

asily forget
its pre-Wagner

ian color-
ing sound

s.

Mirroring

If we could

only see our
selves as o

thers do Mirr
oring more

of their eye-
spent need

s for reali
zing us, so!

For Rosemarie

The sweet
ness of a

kiss flower
s new growth

from this
wintered-

down soil-
of-mine.

Putting this

Humpty-Dumpty

land of our
s back togeth

er again is
like being

puzzled with
all those

black space
s and the un

answering
question

s blank to
their very-

source.

Love

at second

sight (though
slightly en

raptured
from the first)

feeling in
to the depth

of its increa
sing after–

impression
s.

Turtle

s seem best

ly endowed
against

this rush–
flighty

world of our
s slow-pac

ed heavily
kept protect

ively in–
touch with

the ground–
base of all–

such relevant
ly forward

s go-ahead
s.

For Rosemarie

the bait I

took fast–
sinking the

hidden-depth
of a strange

ly occupied
new-world.

134

Snow-

sense time

lessly re
calling

these wind-
swept momen

tarily now
s.

Maundy Thurs

day the un

leavened
bread of

Christ's cru
cified body

long-reclaim
ing those

vast distan
ces of his

disciple
s' wandering

s.

Love

(even after
50 years)

must be read
ily pursued

rather than
enstalled

on a throne
of always–

reigning.

If even

snakes can
shed old skin

s Why can't
we at least

squirm our
selves out

of failed
conviction

s.

Political

poems quick

ly fail-of–
their–time

s But some
lasting re

sidues can
be truthed

to enduring
meaning

s.

Her baby-

black–out–of–

wedlock smil
ing a self–

satisfy
ing "Here I

am whatever
cause may

have birth
ed me."

She knew

it wasn't

the right
way but

there–it–
was flower

ing a grac
ious sense

of life-be
ing.

Kaleb

souled with

"another
spirit" than

the fear–
immersing

eyes of his
God–abandon

ing people.

She

played–by–

ear as if
the musical

depth of her
sound-fing

ered-feel
ings could be

come too eas
ily lifeless

ly papered-
down.

A drab

dead–silent
day bare–bran

ched to the
very root of

its self–deny
ing awaken

ings.

Caged-in

rabbits ear–

lengthing
a carrot'

s world's e
longating

run–jump
s.

A dizzi

ness that

his world
kept turn

ing round
its center

couldn't
be held form

lessly out
going.

Tchaikov

sky's First

Quartet be
gins with a

lyrically
self-involv

ing theme
continual

ly answer
ing its own

self-recall
ings.

Debussy'

s String Quar

tet so indi
vidually

voicing space
and color-

forming.

The string

quartet fam

ily's the
most intimate

ly attuning
personal-pre

sence.

Animals

(each in

theirs own-
way) mirror

ing those un
seen eye

s of our
vaguely

familiar-
felt.

Each friend

inhabit

ing another
side of our

always re
volving

self-find
s.

Chosen

It wasn't

the Israel
of their

time-return
ing dream

s as if
That Israel

of David and
Solomon

hadn't fail
ed as well

(though still
chosen) through

God's unrelent
ing will-

powered.

That natur

al flow-of–
line easing

into a time-
space unity

of increas
ingly lost–

perspect
ives.

Hebbel's (3)

a) Gyges' ring

invisib
ly alive to

the death–
wish of its

Hades–like
shadowing

presence.

b) Why did the

king allow his
so-admired

friend incog
nito to inhab

it his wife'
s beauti

fied though
night-consum

ing presence.

c) Hebbel's

cave-image

Platonic
and yet Saul–

David to its
most ancient

and yet al
ways reviv

ing present.

The cool

darkness

of early
spring's

raining
time down

to its naked
ly withhold

ing sensed-
growth.

With his

hearing fa

ding from
view He sens

ed why word
s reveal

more than
all those out

wardly artifi
cial appear

ances.

Charlie Chaplin'

s a non-per

son real name'
s never dis

covered He
was but he

isn't paper
ed-for-be

ing.

A large

theatre

empty–seat
ing rows of

invisib
ly attent

ive lost ap
pearance

s.

Keeping

up with his

own steps e
choing a

reflect
ive sound–

off.

Georgia O'Keeffe *(Munich, March 8) (9)*

a) Barn with snow (1934)

The closed

window's
unseeing

depth of
snow's silen

ces.

b) A street (1926)

closed-in

from its tower
ing height

s lonely-touch
ed street

light's just
hanging still-

smalled.

c) Some artist

s (as Georgia O-

Keeffe) at their
best when an

atypical
theme approa

ches their
brush-sense

through a
totally una

wared side-
street.

d) Black lilies (1916)

Mondrian-

like space
finely ab

stract time-
sensing.

e) Blue line (1919)

The origin

of smoke'
s invisib

ly light-
sounding

s.

f) Peach and

glass-form

rounding-
out a color

ed sense-in-
being.

g) Red hills I
Lake George (1927)

The slope-

flowing past
sun-light'

s brighten
ed emerg

ings.

h) Red hills II

The sun

as if awak
ening those

soft-realm
s of its

awaiting
lover.

i) Stables (1932)

Horses si

lently en
closing an

unseen there
abouts.

O'Keeffe

landscap

ed dead-
rock into

a living
scope of its

always-
there.

What is

past may

still color–
us–through

a seeing–
sense of the

now-known.

Poems on poem (2)

a) Forerunners

We've all

been set–
loose through

forerunn
ing those

streams of
semi–conscious

ly realized.

b) Instant

poems as

the sudden
ly–there

squirrel'
s thin–in

scaping
line.

A flash

ed image of

a bird shad
owing its

own after
thought

s.

Time-planning

There's
little scope

for time-plan
ning if we'

re still as
sembling as

a bird nest-
wise for its

own shelter
ed self-be

ings.

An Italian in Algiers *(Rossini) (2)*

a) more like

a dance-and-
song routine

Music for
the eyes not

for the ear'
s mind.

b) Curious

ly color
ing staging

those big en
semble num

bers inspir
ing a world

foreign to
ours dense

ly time-
set.

For Rosemarie

All that we

see hear
sense-feel

the more of
our awaken

ing togeth
erness-find

s.

That dark

night at the

Starnberg
er See still

permeating
those wave-

intelling
phases of my

uncertain
ed self-aware

nesses.

In memory George Herbert

Can living-

out the full
ness of this

life curtain
us from that

Christ–given
better one

to come.

These wave

s restless

ly insecur
ing the shore

s of their
home–find

ing return
s.

A living-

elegy He sim

ply left out
of my life

a dear friend
apparent

ly secured
from those un

spoken cultur
al divide

s.

Beyond

He felt him

self drift
ing out a

way into
those silent-

sounds wave-
like increas

ingly beyond.

For Rosemarie

The softness

of a self-real
izing kiss

petals the
touch of those

dark-secret
ly self-enclos

ing realm
s.

Wood-cut-

through

the bared
hands of its

life-compell
ing scent.

The first

time he heard

his own self-
disclosing

voice at the
depth of a

medieval
well echoing

back those
stone-embrac

ing silence
s.

Night driv

ing that phan

tom-feel of
undisclos

ing danger
s looming

within their
own shadow

ing reach.

Hanging grape

s (not those

fox-enchant
ing sour-one

s) but fully
fleshed to a

ripeness
that must be

crushed to
their fresh

ly vintaged
wine-source.

Karl Stamitz

(though plac

ed so inept
ly between

Haydn and Mo
zart) as a

self-enclos
ing wall rare

ly heard out
side its so-

limited con
fines.

The bigger

and better
ness of Ameri

ca's drip-
school left

those fine
ly crafted

artists as
Charles Seli

ger to the
modest little

ness of his
so careful

ly crafted
growth-color

ings.

Identity

A Jew here

a Christian
there And if

he met him
self from

around that
just-arriv

ing corner
mirroring

what or e
ven whom.

Knowing

your true

age (at time
s much young

er–felt than
years could

describe) de
fies those

paper–categor
ies seeing–

sensed.

Meeting Schütz

on his own

perilous
ground of ag

ing year
s and yet

that blood–
rousing rhy

thmic poet
ic urge.

Anti-Semitism'

s a fluctuat

ing virus with
always new

and increas
ingly inaffect

ive vaccine
s for treat

ing its acti
vating cause.

Black

birds myster

iously encir
cling the

outspoken
wood's bared-

down empti
nesses.

They march

ed-off so

admirably
to war with

all their pat
riotic phras

ings until
war settled–

them–down in
to four-star

(though less-
sound-proof)

bunkers.

When dis

ease grasp

s at the
blood-de

signs of
your very–

being less
of that mind–

certain
ed self.

Sleep

less night

moon-awake
to those

very-fear
s inhabit

ing the last
fibre of

your self
lessly phan

tomed being.

Morning'

s subdued
greyness

a lonesome
impending

mood curtain
ed-down self-

enclosing.

Ghiselebertus'

Eve the sen

suous snake-
eyed temptr

ess seduct
ively calling

to a world
of lush-fruit

ed bottom-
pitted bare

nesses.

White-wash

ed houses

left a sens
ed–down im

pression
of those kind

of person
s with espec

ially refur
nished inter

iors.

Night encom

passes the

more of why
we keep sit

ting out the
depth of

those untold
silence

s.

For Norman

living a

dying-unto-
death he

took each
day as if

the last
learning to

see think and
hear what he'

d little-
known before

life had be
come its so

intrinsi
cally self-

awareness.

Dentist

I heard him

(in his mid–
50s) breath

ing hard
close to my

extended face
under the

stress of a
difficult

task as an
old–fashion

ed train puff
ing out the

lesser speed
of an uncer

tained re
solve.

At the dent

ist a real

tree's over
hanging leave

s me as if ex
pressive

ly fashion
ed for its

self–protect
ing presence.

For a woman'

s choice of

dress–taste
becomes a

real life-of–
its-own color

ing the fabr
ic of her pre–

intended
touched-ex

pressive
ness.

"Winter

gardens" as
the captain'

s outlook
distanc

ing more (or
even less)

of his self–
standing

there.

Polonius'

advice better

to say noth
ing while ap

pearing smart
ly-poised

than to be
tracked

through a
landscape

hardly map
ed-out for

your furtive
self-esteem

ing message.

The snow

didn't come

however in
tensely our

need-felt
for its time-

relieving
soothing

ly purify
ing distan

ces.

Pain *(3)*

a) Answer

ing pain's dead
ly determin

ing darts
best express

ed not by a
careful

ly thought–
through the

sis But the
way Dürer

sought its
respite encir

cling exact
ly the pene

trating place
of its dead

ly unabat
ing origin

s.

b) Pain'

s that short-

way trip be
tween life

and death'
s calling us

to its god
ly need for

comfort
ing now and

always–then.

c) Pain

lessens

most by
grasping

hold of
Christ's

nailed–in
claims–for–

us Crucifi
ed without

relief
from pain–

soothing
wine.

N. S.

on both side

s of most
every argu

ment smiling
the softly-

fleshed ap
pearance

of the peace-
maker's sover

eign Christ
ianity.

Wood

pecker's

hammering
its wood-

tighten
ed rhythm

ic cause as
my dentist'

s vibrat
ing each tooth'

s defective
ly-worn ca

sings.

A minor quartet *(Mendelssohn, last mvt.)*

The first move

ments should
have been left

untouched to
their self–

finishing
sensed–fine

nesses.

Visions fugitives *(Prokofiev-Barshai)*

Quick to ex
press as if

skating on
ice–surfac

ing its hid
den withhold

ing depth
s.

Mendelssohn'

s A Minor Quar
tet at the

death of Beet
hoven quoting

his master
time-and-a

gain sound
ing just-

like him
self.

A young and

able quartet-

group program
med (very un

Russian like)
works of ton

ed-down less
er-felt short

ly-confined
classical ex

pressive
ness.

When the

pain reced

ed numbed
from its con

tinual there
ness He felt

a–sense–of–
loss as if

bodied to a
somewhere

's more–than–
himself.

The morning

took–him–by–

surprise
Too bright

to realize
his aging

needs for
slowed–down a

wareness
es.

"6th piano concerto"

as if those

5 Beethov
ian piano con

certi weren'
t enough for

that eager
young pianist

outstripp
ing the gen

uine violin
tone and tim

bre to his
appreciat

ing foreign–
fingered pian

istic skill
s.

Poems from Schwanberg *(Franconia) (17)*

a) Enclosed

within the

confines of
a Rennaiss

ance castle
he awoke to

a time-bet
ween-time

s world
left him

but a trans
parent i

mage through
his scarce

ly inhabit
ed self.

b) Spring was

"in-the-air"

though only
slightly

witness
ing its deli

cately earth–
touched color

ings.

c) Old build

ings however
beautiful

ly remember
ing a time

when the Jew–
in–me fear

ed for his
very-ghetto

ed being.

d) He realiz

ed the sub
tle almost

thought-in
voking a

sides of
that still

spring morn
ing's true

expressive
ness.

e) Do ancient

walls as

these reveal
their time-e

luding se
crets through

such innocent
ly appearing

facades.

f) That glass

open-land

elevator
lifted us

far beyond
the height

of our reali
zing where.

g) Branch

es budded

with a seld
om length

of delicate
color-find

s.

h) The if-quest

ions may not
appear histor

ically sound
though they

continue to
enhance the

other-sided
ness of what

actually
happened.

i) Dark only

became that

because
the night had

taken-hold
of his en

tire thought–
felt being.

j) The invisi

ble winds

swayed the
night bran

ches to the
rhythmic

flow of
their un

known myster
ious source.

k) Little

in-bred Renn

aissance wind
ows mirror

ing the self-
enclosing

life of the
successive

Counts of Cas
tell-Rüden

hausen.

l) He listen

ed to the

night–silen
ce until he

realized
that silen

ce was lis
tening

through him.

m) Those wind

ing stair

s may have
direction

ed his life
until at the

top he reali
zed the full–

bottomness
of his self–

pursuing
claims.

n) Only while

kneeling

under the
full-weight

of that cath
edral's

towering
claims did

he realize
the very-

littleness
of his God-

denying way
s.

o) Barren

once fruit-

bearing tree
s exposing

the lost-
find's time

lessness of
this ever-

aging cast
le.

p) The land

scaping

Francon
ian distan

ces of his
life's full

ness of e
ver-renew

ing poetic
vistas.

q) It was

his own foot
steps that

left shad
ows behind

as if a
weight had

been taken
from the step

s of his e
choing-be

yondness.

A group

of aging wo

men encirc
ling an unre

1ifed lone
liness a

common voice
that could be

listening
through e

ver-distin
ctly to

their own.

Two birds

(small one

s) mating
an open-voice

d unison at
my window

still tremb
ling at the

source of
their birth–

encompass
ing desire

s.

These bared

branches

budding at
seldom inter

vals life'
s through-re

claiming
source.

Rain-

pearls birth

ed in the
aftermath

of night'
s delicate

ly releas
ing touch.

He gave

one that all-

nice-and-
cozy-feeling

as if life
had been sofa

ed to the
comforts of

those so
soft-relaxing

smiles of
his.

On the brink

A world liv

ing on that
Titanic-brink

fully unaware
of that dead

ly-floating
iceberg hidd

en beneath
the dark of

their unknow
ing where.

A cool-moist

day sensing
the earthy

closeness
of why his

thoughts
seemed so

heavily re
mote.

Miscplaced

Invited

though mis
placed al

most invis
ibly passed-

by self-sha
dowing.

No word

from him for

weeks as a
skier lost

from snow–
sight to that

perilous
depth of not–

finding
where.

Snow

drops inno

cently touch
ing through

their so
modest way

of speak
ing scarce

ly aloud.

When it

started cloud

ing up
that even

the moon seem
ed vaguely

light-compell
ing.

Gyges' ring *(Hebbel) (continued) (9)*

d) Have we

lost our
sense-of-shame

clothed in ap
pearance

s though na
ked at the

heart of our
primitive

ly "natural"
sense-of-be

ing.

e) The pathos

of these death–

cried ending
s (though ori

gined in the
plot) seem

ed almost
humourous

ly–aestheti
cally off–bal

ancing.

f) The king'

s servant

true not
only to that

king but e
ven to his

blood–espous
ing now crown–

bearing succes
sor.

g) A Greek-

like chorus

of only two
young lady–

courtier
s encircl

ing this stead
ily self–con

suming blood–
thirsted

tragedy.

h) Hebbel'

s finely

spaced rhetor
ically even–

stanced though
not–really

"archaic"
ally compell

ing sense–
for–theatre.

i) Good play

s don't preach

(as the minist
er-son Less

ing would
have us be

lieve) But
they do touch

somewhere
within cer

tain special
ly dressed-o

ver realm
s of oursel

ves and of
our time

s.

j) How much

of our be

ing invisib
ly ringed

to those
self-conceal

ing realm
s of pre-

existence.

k) Tradition

s may have "for

ced us" to
act against

our "true in
terests"

But without
them we're a

drift help
lessly alone

d.

l) It all be

gan (the

real germ of
this tragedy

as with the
biblical Book

of Esther) when
the queen re

fuses to
display her

called
self public

ally.

A new day

>as an empty
>
>page to be
>written full
>
>but mostly
>inwardly
>
>conceived
>between
>
>its preestab
>lishing
>
>lines.

Does a

>king need
>
>the symbol
>of a crown
>
>to appear
>more than he
>
>has actual
>ly become.

Is the min

ister's gown

(those black
ones) a way

of clothing
him within

the darken
ed realms

of Christ'
s redeeming

cross.

"A chair"

The universi

ties called
it "a chair"

though not
one to be

sat upon with
the weight

of one's heav
ily embrac

ing thought
s.

Daylight sav

ing's time as

if man had be
come the mast

er of his
own days

(those hour
s and minute

s) still re
volving their

same speed and
equally plann

ed length-of-
day.

Complete

Is a poem

only then com
plete when

it's found the
length and dep

th of its own
pre-conceiv

ing form.

Squirrelled

Our tree-in
habiting

squirrel
put on his

whole acroba
tic show of

leaps jump
s and slen

der branch
ed-aside

s to impress
us (or him)

with a dis
play of squirr

elled agility.

Framed

Is the frame

of a picture
its own pre

conceived
way of a lim

iting stop–
here Or should

its form
and color

ed-enclosing
a unity of

samed–sense.

Terminab

ly ill he

needed a
cause to keep

his life cen
tered away

from its ul
timately

self–consum
ing end.

Does the

writing of

these poem
s in the

early–morn
ing hours im

ply the
poetic voice

awakened–
a brightness

from its dark
ly withhold

ing shadow
ed–origin

s.

After Psalm 39

He knew he

needed some
thing more

even when
death would

become the
final voice

of its life–
urging claim

s.

Are we but

two selves

tensioned
at the un

heard sha
dow–spread of

time's illu
sively self–

becoming
s.

Tiger Wood'

s a phantom

of life's
off-the-course

still inhabit
ing the rhy

thmic urge
of its very-

swing.

As a child

grown into a

woman's age
She hadn't

yet been
taught to

conceal
that first–

felt most–
of-her.

"Prince-of-this-world"

Who's "the

prince-of–
this-world"

's satanic
realms or

Christ hidd
en in the dark

of his self–
pursuing

claims.

Man's

more like a

play-cat un
ravelling

the folds
of his cloth–

binding in
stinct

s.

Gypsy Ma

donna of early

Titian romanti
cally color

ing out the
classical

ly self-with
holding blue–

for-the-pur
ity of Bellini'

s pre–existent
Godly order.

Do the

first spring

flowers se
cretly deep

en their col
ors into the

cool of the
moon's encom

passing light.

The Jewish way

Religious

books how
ever agèd–

from–use must
be kept a–

live as the
touched gar

ments of
those ever–pre

sent saint
ly relics.

Two-levelled

A two-levell

ed life
(as in Grand

Central Stat
ion) climb

ing the step'
s discover

ies of that
time-inclusive

ly distanc
ing from that

other–sense–
of-self.

If climate-

change doesn'

t really im
ply a like

wise change-
of-person

as that pale
Polish Jew

now darkly be
coming the

biblical
ly-proud

war-stanc
ed Israel

i.

When 54 % of

these-day

Germans real
ly believe

that Israel
treats their

Arabs as Hitl
er the Jews

then Goebbel'
s still right

ing-himself
through the

repeating
lies penetrat

ing to the une
qualled

depth of
lie-truth

s.

Today'

s freedom

to believe
what you've

been taught
to be true

may free
each-of-us

from that ang
ling decision

to self-de
cide.

History

may not re

peat itself
But it's al

ways there
lying dormant

ly ready to
reveal its

nakedly un
masking de

signs.

Dohnányi

Serenade op. 10

took me
right in

to the "swing-
of-things"

perhaps heard
before but

still com
pletely-

yours.

The "almost

best friend"

movied why
we all need

a complemen
tary-self to

fully real
ize the mean

ing of our
own.

Robert

do you remem

ber at Play
land how we

roller-coast
ed the height

of our fear
s downed into

the dark-chasm
ed inside-

outs.

Spring (3)

a) is like an

undecided
woman Should

she or should
she not bloom

ed with those
first beautify

ing blossom
ings would

soon fade in
to their in

decisive
earthy claim

s-on-her.

b) Spring'

s almost

too pretty
(as a young

girl first
ly colored-

clothed) to
remain endur

ingly so it
repeatedly

changes the
direction

of our not
long-for hold

ing.

c) Spring'

s undecid

edly longing
for its sum

mer fulfill
ment may for

get (as the
later roman

tics) the pur
ity of its

firstly-con
ceived.

Dvorak

my first a

dolescent
love modulat

ing the ac
cords of

those still
not so self–

attuned a
wakening

s.

Can silence

grow as flow

ers color
ing for the

light of
these wind–

shifting mo
ments.

A false–

start off be

fore runn
ing those self–

encircling
lonelin

ness re
turn

s.

Keiser'

s pre–Bach'
s Mark Passion

classical
ly condens

ing those es
sential trans

parencies
of textual–

sound.

Danger

lurks most–

deeply with
in the hidden

recesses of
our own

scarce
ly reali

zing self–
being.

Grass-

flower
s as if

still un
heard why

they're so
separate

ly light-cho

sen.

An old friend

for good rea

son banished
out of my con

suming past
sitting there

on the same
sofa he'd left

for-the-last-
time as if

time-itself
had become re

conciled to
its own encom

passing sense-
for-forgetful

ness.

"I've seld

om met a
young man as

nice as this
one" Words

from a former
SS killer

who would have
killed me

right-on-the
spot of my

Jew-being.

If (as Jesus

implied) we'll

be judged the
same way we'

ve judged o
thers then e

ven a close-mouth
ed awareness

will shut-down
on us at its

very-end.

"I'm not

guilty" her

first sign-of-
reaction to

my Jew-being
blameless

ly new-start
as if time'

s only resolv
ed for its

futurable
needs.

Poems for Wolfi (4)

a) They'd liv

ed here be

fore the
house worn

with the
faded foot-

prints of
their timed-

out vacanc
ies.

b) Can a friend

ship broken-

off years be
fore be newly in

habited with
a changing

sense of be
coming now

(and no-where
s-else).

c) To realize

anew that

even the SS
(using un

armed Jews
for target-

practice)
were really

humaned
flesh and blood

discolor
ing.

d) That third-of-a-Jaffin

He discover

ed that third-
of-a-Jaffin

liberal Jew
ish histor

ian biblical
Christian

and now a
poet daily re

viving life'
s (hidden from

itself's) dis
coverie

s.

Why redis

cover a mined-

past danger
˙ed at every

step with
those over

whelming
times of e

very sense
of self-be

ing.

To believe

what one

wants–to–be
lieve implie

s a more–than–
harmless re

dunancy bet
ween cause

and effect.

Sleep'

s the wave–

clouding
of our unre

vealed shore
s–approach

ings.

His usual way

It was his u

sual way of
asking more

question
s than could

be possibly
answered in

to a mosaic

of weaving-

through co
loring de

signs.

Bruckner's 9th (4)

a) strange

ly beautify

ing dissonant'
s silver-sens

ing as the
magic touch

of rarely
seen seclud

ed flower
s.

b) Formless

ly overlong

as a stage
always revolv

ing back to
where it wasn'

t anymore.

c) Bombasti

cally sancti

fying Wagner'
s dangerous

ly heroic
claims.

d) When space

opens–out

to those majest
ic fields ly

rically pulse–
sensing.

History

may not re

peat itself
though it

can be turn
ed as a glob

ous coming
back to more

(or less)
of the same

place and time.

If the Jew

s were "the

source of our
own misfort

une" then
killing them

off blooded
the depth of

that alway
s self-retain

ing source.

Many family-

trees here

sanctify
some of those

rotten bran
ches that need

be cut-off to
retain a con

tinuous
ly healthy

growth.

An unexpect

ed meeting

that off-bal
anced what

ever compos
ure he could

n't prepare
to a sit-down

face-finding
s.

Buried

medieval

gold jewed
to a blood-

depth of its
timeless

ly reclaim
ing inherit

ance.

They brought

the self-in

criminat
ing facts to

life after
the guilty had

been buried in
the peaceful

solitude of
their time-in

gratiating
graveyard

s.

We can't un

do what's al

ready been
done But at

least we can
knot it tight

to its breath
less end.

Unhistorical Questions *(4)*

a) Does our art

reveal the in

ner dimension
s of self Or

is it care
fully poised

at the other
end of our

unknown be
ing simply

there of its
own accord

s.

b) Does lesser-

known art as

that of Vermeer
or Georges de

la Tour become
fully accepted

only when the
time-view has

become closer
to that of

their-own.

c) Without the

great "teach

ers" as Pushkin
Corelli Haydn

or Bellini
would those

epochs have re
mained stati

cally remote.

d) Two ways of

"understand
ing" great art

The technical
ly-adept pro

fessional
one Or the

more intuit
ive poetic

way.

Relativism

Seeing from-
all-sides his

torically-re
newing may

(at times)
correct the

cycloptic
oneness of

"mine's the
only way"

(but then)
we've only

two eyes for
seeing what

may have its
own distinct

ive way-for-
meaning.

Thought-

poems (how

ever necess
ary) may think-

us but until
They've left

those poem
s bared-to

their own
poetic sense-

for-being.

That run-a

way bear

may have been
surround

ed from all-
sides (but

still) it
found its own

way (perhaps
a 5th side)

for slipp
ing past their

all-encompass
ing reach.

"The whole

truth and noth

ing but the
truth" as if

the truth
wasn't separ

ately eye-match
ed for each

of our own
(often color–

blind) per
spective

s.

The more

he read over

his own poem
s as if he'

d become too
much a part

of them to o
ver-see what

they hadn't
realized be

fore.

Corelli *(on his 300ᵗʰ birthday)*

that master–

maker of Baro
que forms

left–his–mark
more on his

own follow
ers than on

time's stingy
way of reveal

ing again the
abstract–pur

ity of his so
classical

ly compress
ed creation

s.

Transcendings *(3)*

a) Trio Hb. 29 (Haydn)

When a mast
er–of–form

transcend
ing a new sen

sibility well–
beyond phras

ing it just–
right.

b) Ravel'

s trio mood–

tones an out
door interior

world time-
transcend

ing even its
brighten

ed shadow
ings.

c) Schubert'

s last great

trio balanc
ing dramatic–

poetical
ly transcend

ing a world
of his final

farewell
s.

When you'

re deeply

tired the
world remain

s as a sunk
en ocean rare

ly lifted to
its sail–boat

surfacing
s.

Main-

streams oft

so direct
ioned that

its elusive
source become

s slow–bound
wider than

its feeding-
tributar

ies could
possibly fresh

en–through.

No signs-

of–life they

lay there
as if dead

even T. V.–im
mune to their

motionless
ly lived–out

life.

At almost

90 alone with

a private
room's increas

ing view dis
tancing bare-

ground her
life-long re

membrance
s.

Gauguin'

s Arcarea

strange
ly statical

ly alive to
the muted tone

s of her time-
awakening

flute-calling
s.

She wore

her Sunday-

best ornament
ing a some

how adorning
respect for

the naked Christ
clothed in noth

ing but His
pains and blood-

depth.

For the first-time

If life's

always for
the first-

time's real
poetry replac

ing a routine
daily-same

ness touched-
even-sensed.

John Stuart Mill

saved from

his father'
s deaden

ing upbring
ing-grasp

ed through
the still liv

ing grace
of goodly en

riching ro
mantic

poetry.

Fighting

on even more

than two front
s may lessen

his ammunit
ion's aimed–

certainty un
til emptied–

down to the
nothing-left

but that lost–
feeling of

voiceless
impotence.

Puppet

s may become

an answer
ing back to

what was
only really

asked through
those self-

attending eye
s of her most

ly-repeating
always-reassur

ing partial
ly-smiled.

A fearful

middle-sized

tail-down-fold
ing-dog from a

keep-them-well-
alive kennel

looking sheep
fully misplac

ed in the
midst of fam

ilied reassure
ing love-pat

s.

H. M.

Jobless
ly six-child

rened joined
the SS' s e

litist sense-
of-self-import

ance Shot him
self repeated

ly into his
own soulless

self-shadow
ings.

A Conductor's appraisal

It was the
train that

kept them
there nameless

ly inhabit
ing less space

than their
fears could

voiceless
ly resound

it took
them there

day-by-day
samed-tracked

to their end–
stopped dis

posals.

The first

spring-leave

s freshly ap
pearing as

if almost
touched–

through
their birth

ed–silence
s.

He usual

ly embraced

(mostly smil
ing) both side

s of a quest
ion A high

churchman
lowered to

the pleasan
tries of a

self-imposing
tolerance.

Questioning Goethe

Feelings

(then) might
be justified

through their
freshly ex

pressing it
requires (per

haps) today a
subtle-realiz

ing their in
wardly-attun

ed self-express
iveness.

Nuance

s of new

ly express
ed feeling

(s) us
through the

colored en
closure

s of however
sensed vivid

ly landscap
ings.

2nd Commandment *(Moses)*

As one of
those magneti

cally-encom
passing per

sons She shap
ed her child

ren and those
reached within

her encircl
ing domain

s in the i
mage of her

own sensed-con
suming per

son.

Overly large

black-involv
ing birds

circling
the woods in

the darkness
es of their

own deeply
sourced-from

being.

Eyes too

closely search

ing the very-
depth of his

unexplor
ed oceaned

bottom-grou
nd.

García

Lorca's Blood–

Marriage
densely color

ed in the
poetry of ar

chaic blood–
intensing se

quence
s.

Wallace Notestein

(as they warn
ed me)

may have turn
ed every con

versation in
to his new

ly-coming
book carpet-

cleaning
all those

left-over un
certain

ties.

Foot-noting

He may have

realized in
time the

many foot-
notes to his

usually un
resolving

person
ed those bott

om-pages in
closely self-

defining
print.

Revision

istic histor

ians may not
have alter

ed the fact
s but the

focus of our
reading their

intricate
ly side-street

ing length
s.

Blood marriage (García Lorca) (4)

a) The poetry

of theatre
when nature'

s become vis
ibly a-part-

of-our-own
callings for

blood and the
darkness of

death's over
coming instin

cts.

b) When true

stories be
come even tru

er-told vivid
ly recalling

deadly-alive.

c) Evil curr

ents it own

blood–path–
passions the

love-death
of more than

even "good
blood" and

tradition'
s length

could possib
ly endure.

d) Ezekiel 18

If I'm only

me and noth
ing more-or-

less Why have
past-time

s often
caught–us–

up in their
continuing

fateful-de
signs.

Communist

Germany's

samed–new
cities Eyed

with more
than even

those out–
staring win

dows could
transpar

ently real
ize.

"How far can one go"

>in a controll

>ed society'
>s also a

>question of
>realizing

>that other–side
>of one's own

>secretly dark
>ening in–tuned

>self.

Does the

>blank canvas

>conceal a–
>voice–of–its–

>own realiz
>ing its pre

>colored de
>signs.

With night-

seeing eye

s he owled
the moon in

to his soul
ed semi-dark

nesses.

The pull of

the graveyard'

s down-to-earth
calling this

minister-
poet stone-

on-stone re
clusive

ly side-fac
ed.

Lamentation *(Symphony 26, Haydn minuet)*

A strange con

cluding move
ment's dance-

macabre's rhy
thmic shadow

ings.

1st *Piano Concerto I* *(Bach)*

the quick

movement
s rhymed more

to their own
need for a

non–stopp
ing pause.

1st *Piano Concerto II* *(Bach, slow movement)*

spacious

ly opening
the heaven

ly depth of
creation'

s time-touch.

Symphony 7 *(Dvořák)*

rhythmic

ally sensed
to a predeter

mining end–
start.

7th *Symphony* (Dvořák)

piccolo'

s repeated
clash-shiv

ering light-
swells tragic

ally aware
d.

Günter Grass

self-appoint

ed SS moral
apostle pre

sanction
ing Israel'

s defense
less death-

ends.

These night-

    darkening

    trees loom
    ing ever high

    er than e
    ven the solemn

    winds in
    creasing

    ly voiced.

La Valse (Ravel 1914)

    The Titanic

    ship-of-fool
    s gold-gild

    ing its trea
    sured appear

    ances under-
    watered

    struck-down
    to a depth

    of increas
    ing darkness

    es.

The Christic-passover

"Why is this

night differ
ent from e

very other
night" because

Christ took-
it–on as His

own All–impend
ing darkness

the fear of
death's over

riding cause
d through

His redeem
ing fleshed–

blooded
ness.

Each nail

ed–in moment

Upstanding
His bod

ied–poised
to that inde

scribable
length of

crucifying
blood–bless

ings.

"I thirst"

Christ at

the bottom-
breath of His

dried–out bod
ied–cry for

the life-
source of

death–over
coming

s.

"That is your

mother That is
your son"

as if a new
family–in–

faith was
called–into–

being rarely
sanctified

above the old
er blood–re

lated one.

An empty

road disappear
ing into the

wood's depth
of hidden si

lences.

The cold wea

ther hasn't

loosened
its deaden

ing grasp on
these naked

ly-gnarled
wintered bran

ches.

St. John Passion *(Bach)*

classical

ly-close
ly phrased

to but a sin
gle predeter

mined route
All voiced to

that end-of-
the-line's e

ternal destin
ation – Golga

tha.

Aging

Some part of

us more used-
out than o

thers almost
an incomplet

ed person ran
domly pain-

dressed.

She was

    80 and her

    eyes still
    looked young

    perhaps be
    cause she had

    rarely wit
    nessed the real

    unpleasant
    ries of life

    or because
    her husband'

    s death still
    contemplat

    ing with its
    renewal call

    ings for liv
    ing-it-out.

A bush

    so profuse

    ly yellow
    that it seem

    ed as if the
    sun had flow

    ered-down its
    radiant bright

    ly self-con
    suming fire.

It snowed

the Easter

night through
that overcom

ing depth of
darkness leav

ing behind
only a white-

encompass
ing sense-of-

purity.

Doubting Thomas (*Caravaggio*)

Only then

at that very-
moment did the

flesh-depth
of touch trans

forming in
to those un

touchable
realms of

spirit.

On that time

lessly envelop

ing road to
Damascus

St. Paul blind
ed with the

divine light
of creation'

s self-trans
forming route

(root) cause.

Ionesco

When the ab

surd truth of
a self-involv

ing world lead
s to a no-

way-out He'
ll be waiting

at the open
ing light of

that exit-
door.

Fresh

ly imprint

ing that new–
fallen snow

with first–
felt light–in

stinct
s.

This late-

light snow as

if a remind
er of those

unremember
ed time's re

vealing past.

Early Titian *(via Giorgione)*

romantiz
ing Bellini'

s classical
ly time–sus

pending world.

Noli Me Tangere *(Titian)*

so beautify

ing Christ's
time-escap

ing world of
our touching

to hold-true
to that un

touchably in
becoming

world of His.

Titian

when colors

became so
densely self–

appealing
that not e

ven cloth or
flesh could

long-hold
their so pro

fusely time
lessness.

On this

cold spring–

winter day
The sun's mut

ed light as
a voice no

longer fully
aware of its

self-resound
ing depth.

No one

allowed to

witness the
unearthly re

surrection
except that

celestial
God-bespok

en light-an
gel and those

brought-to-
life stones

fully surpris
ed by their

through-
touching a

wakening
s.

Repeat

    ing the same

    theme's like
    a sculpture

    rotating
    the hand–

    length of
    its redefin

    ing surface
    s.

Her husband

    slowly dy

    ing her face–
    fading in

    to that last
    resonance

    of timed–
    freshness.

He heard

    his own voice

    from afar
    like listen

    ing through
    the ocean

s depths si
lently await

ing a mess
age scar

cely indeciph
erably heard.

Self-proclaim

ing moralist

s as Günther
Grass-rooted

to that bitt
er past he

so often con
vincely dis

claimed.

Van Goyen *(for Tony)*

cloud-creat

ing a surfac
ing depth of

the ocean'
s apparent

stillness
es.

Ode à Frederick Jackson Turner

Is America'

s true heri
tage of its

diverse Eur
opean source

s Or of a
land vacant

ly stretch
ing beyond

even the grow
th of its

pioneer
ing past.

Alena at age 10

She appear

ed dressed
as through

a collage of
so many in

spiring co
lors that one

could have ta
ken her for a

circus-clown
just readied

for her dance-
and-song rout

ine.

When a

young girl'

s spontane
ous playful

ness ripen
s into a

self-withhold
ing sense of

her own inner-
quietude

s.

In memory G. G.

When middle-

age women
more-or-less

realizing
their upbring

ing-children'
s a mostly

lost cause
turn most

emphatical
ly to their un

witting hus
band's need for

a re-doing
polished and

shined to dail
y duty-re

spons
es.

Illmensee

where these

smooth wave
s calming

the reticent
winds into a

conscious
ness of their

time–releas
ing shore

s.

Does a

good poem

teach us an
awareness

of those un
spoken but

still–last
ing touch–

sensing
sounds.

Rain

drops as

slight mo
mentary

ily recurr
ing thought

s increas
ing the in

quietude
s of this

window's
sound

less view.

Clouds

deeply involv

ing a contin
uously world-

changing
sense-of-

their-own.

Can eye

s really ex

press the
soul of our

most inti
mate thought

s.

Aging-

tiredness

daily reminds
us that sleep

and death
are becoming

closely-comm
only sourc

ed.

Thinking deep

er as a well
watered-down

to the very-
depth of its

stone-suport
ive foundat

ion.

Woodcarver

Winter car

ved his hand
s and the

intensity
of his eye'

s reach in-to
the grained

source of
that wood'

s rhythmic-
impulsing

s.

It froze a

gain down in-

to his in
stinctual

need for
light-aware

nesses.

Last Phase (2)

a) Towards

the end he

became ever
lesser-weight

ed to the
completing

image of his
name's re

sounding
call.

b) When distan

ces became
the–more–of–

him than e
ven his shad

ow's indis
tinct self–

certain
ty.

Spring

There's some

thing of a
young girl'

s pleasur
ably design

ed lightly
flowered

fabric of
her first

spring dress
ed to her

half-awaken
ing inner ac

cords.

Roads

once built

from pre-con
ceiving de

signs read
ily reclaim

ing a famil
iar distance

of their own
time-envelop

ing intent.

Rebirth

when those

frozen-down
streams as

if called
from a dis

tant voice
loosening

their intense
wintered

hold-on that
renewing

poetic pulse.

Rosemarie

as some wo

men may sub
tlely imply

a change–of–
dress rearrang

ing a commun
ity of inner

self–accord
s.

Little-fat-

lonely–boy

stool–sitting
each day'

s sadly
satisfy

ing look and
an equally

reclusive
left–handed

hamburger.

With him

one must care

fully secure
a distance

to one's own
spontane

ous response
as a nose-

following
dog leashed-

on-to its
duty-accord

ed space-
reach.

Late romantic

symphonic-
bombast as

the increas
ing depth of

overswell
ing storm-

clouds left
him clutch

ing his lit
tle-spaced

lone-chair
ed inquiet

udes.

Pink

in one of

those bloss
oming moment

s of his
collecting

multi-color
ed orchid'

s through
his sublime

ly enchant
ing smiled-

face.

No where

to go from

this sky-in
clusive

sameness
of darkly in

truding o
ver-cast mo

ment's sit-
downs.

My father

never made

it young
as the eldest

always respon
sible that

children
ran around

his imagin
ary never-hav

ing-been try
ing to feel

like what he'
d never felt

before.

A lone

bird solitary
sitting-out

branches of
spaced silen

ces.

Self-Portrait

He acclaim

ing so many-
sided as a

tentacled Oct
opus ink-cen

tered.

My father

only became

child–like
after his

fall took
him down to

a mind–simpli
city help

less but still
promising.

273

They new

ly appraised

their friend
s according

to the dollar-
and-cent worth

of their look
ed-up stored

(even cost re
ducing)

values.

This window

may always
see-it-samed

But I've been
mirrored

through its
reflective

shadow
ing self-con

templation
s.

These cloud

    s so light

    ly blue an
    innocence

    of still un
    touching

    transpar
    encies.

The Rite of Spring *(Stravinsky)*

    thirst

    ing a prim
    itive-animall

    ed urge earth
    y-darkly

    self-inhabit
    ing.

With callous

hands and a

surging will
He split that

virgined
wood to the

depth of its
ingrained

unbaring
scent-de

sires.

Spring'

s swarming

pluralit
ies of fish

delight
ing their un

seen color-sur
facings.

Lionness

To admire

that command
ing pose of

her readi
ness for a

most unfemale–
like attack

to the blood–
flesh of a

friendly in
nocent grass–

grazing ani
mal isn't to

like the ne
cessity of

what she'
s all-about.

The ease of

watching

through glass
the waves

calmly sens
ing the time

less depth
of these wind–

drifting
thought

s.

Violin Concerto 1 *(Haydn)*

The violin

soulful
ly intun

ing the vast
reach of its

spaceless
ly involv

ing voice.

Violin Concerto 3 *(Haydn, last mvt.)*

as a spider

spinning
the finely–

touched web–
treads of its

momentary
taste-inclin

ations.

The Fall of Man *(7)*

a) Man's his

only natural
enemy but by

far the most
dangerous

of all hidd
en in the dark

est thicket
of his mind'

s inescapab
ly poising a

gainst all
those laws

(written or
not) that

would limit
his own self-

devouring in
stinct

s.

b) Apollonic

art's a per

fect means
of cleans

ing man of
all those pre–

supposing
inner dark

nesses.

c) The Adams and Eves

bit that

first untouch
able fruit

down to the
pitted core

of their own
unsatiable

desire
s.

d) And then

came that un

seen voice
calling them

back from
their irrever

sible way
ward off–bal

ancings.

e) Man's ter

minably dis

eased from
the bitter

root that
tastes his

insatiab
ly blemish

ed–urging
s.

f) Pink

always tak

en with his
most noble

self–imagin
ings dress

ed in the
brightest

of clothed
cover–up

coloring
s.

g) Is the

freshness

of spring'
s first

green inno
cently bear

ing an un
timely re

membrance
of a sym

bol of The
Lord's still

–purifying
gracious

ness.

This wood-

grained desk
repeatly

running-
through its

pre–design
ed self–becom

ing word-
sense.

Desert

time's liv

ing each
day without

need of pre
paring as if

it could be
the last al

ways–in–wait
ing.

Make-up

as music

transform
ed beyond

its origin
al intent

Making the
better of

what's al
ready self–

complete.

Wagner'

s grandiose

self-appreciat
ing statue

boxed–in for
the winter

Nothing but
wood and si

lence as if
the Bayreuth

of the 1920s
and 30s could

n't blood–
through its

Jewish–hate
untimely here–

and–now.

A. B. "in

love with the

law" as he
put his over-

bite exten
sive-smiling

glass–image
s with no o

ther loves
left wife and

children money
and school con

tacts.

This city

shadowing

the more of
his left-be

hind stone-
fantasie

s and too ap
parent step-

balancing
concern

s.

"For-the-birds"

Man–made bird

houses perhaps
s articulat

ing one's own
need for do

mestic in
flying

s.

Martin

imitating

that well-
known Schwab

ian thrift
fulness (him

self being one-
of-that-kind)

presented us
tongue-in-

cheek for our
Golden Anniver

sary with a
single spec

ially hand-
cut flower

bending under-
the-weight of

all his minis
terial's modest

ly bowing
s.

Right-on-the-head

Hitting a

nail right-
on-the-head

splinter
ing much of

those side-
causing peri

pheral damage

s.

Because

time chan
ges even

the mean
ing of its

own as a roller-
coaster heighten

ing-up those
fearful

down-drop
s.

Light-heart

ed poems may

lower the im
pending blood-

pressure's ris
ing-concern

s for a world
muchly out of

its pre-given
orbit.

That soft-

sense of snow

peaceful
ly complet

ing the self-
enclosing

width of his
eye's far-

timed reach.

Rabbit

s inholding
the warmth–

depth of
their blood'

s so innocent
ly fleshed–

through.

Rabbit'

s upstand

ing ears list
ening through

the breath–span
of their a

wared silen
ces.

He didn't

know how he

knew as he
slept through

the moon's full–
light calling

his dreams
out of their

darkly contin
uous flow.

Teinted

windows as

if protect
ing against

the naked
eye's self–

revealing.

"The rest is silence"

only when the

play has liv
ed out its

shadowing
oncoming mask

ed–appearan
ces.

Poem's

a birthplace

as the first
spring flow

er's hesitant
light–awaken

ings.

"Pastoral" Piano Sonata op. 28 *(Beethoven)*

Spaced-in

tervals
thought-down

to their
very touched–

instinct
ual sound.

"Waldstein" Sonata *(Beethoven)*

The brillian

ce of C major
crystal-shining

a dynamic of
classical clar

ities.

A still-

life with fruit

clothed in
the silence

s of untouch
ed pre-form

ing space-col
orings.

Mozart's Piano Sonata K. 311

as if orna

menting a sur
face-agree

ment between
those appre

ciating
realms of

touched-
sound.

Spring'

s that sur

prise season
as if its

finely-felt
first-color

ings being o
verheard a

loud.

That over-

dressed lady

with the o
pera glass

es as if
finger-see

ing's the
true express

ion of a re
fined musical
ity.

Pianist *(for S. L.)*

s most always

s love Chopin'
s pre-destin

ed real marr
iage of fin

gered-sensi
bilitie

s.

If words

don't tell

it just-right
ly formed in

to a pre-es
tablishing

need for cer
tained-ex

pression.

He somehow

had known
an in

creasing
flow-of-bird

s had pass
ed overnight

as he awoke
to but their

faintly-touch
ed shadow

ings.

Dialects *(for H. S.)*

Do dialect

s reveal the
true charact

er of their
so-person

ed outlast
ing express

ion.

Last night

Dick Crews

died over my
telephone

but still
lives about

55 years ear
lier if only

as a pre–dat
ed image of

what he may
have actual

ly become.

Katy

trying to do

mesticate
an ever–so–

fearful Gre
cian street–

dog still hunt
ing for una

wared bird
s it might

take–in from
her own hurr

ied–up need–
s–for–flight.

Spring'

s up and

downs as those
young girl

s on the
swings of

their over-
reaching

time-illus
ions.

Landscaped *(for H. S.)*

she became

from her pre-
determin

ing ground-
sourced S

wabian begin
nings.

That entic

ing Greek

young lady
dressed-in

allusive
but scarce

ly self-de
fining contem

plation
s.

If

he rarely re

peated him
self It's be

cause that
merry-go-wheel

ing him aloft
to those still

untouched star-
sensing

s.

Were those

the girl-e

yes of a not
yet ripen

ing smile
Or of a wo

man's tempt
ing-through

their half-
innocent come-

ons.

1ˢᵗ *Quartet (Janáček)*

mining-out

his rock-im
pregnated

silver-depth
ed source

s.

Janáček

tension

ed an anti
thetic self-

rehears
ing marriage-

dual.

298

Great Fugue op. 133

Beethoven'

s unprettied
rhythmic–

clashing
the depth of

his over
lasting in

terior
claim

s.

After the

Janáček and

Beethoven'
s classical–

upending
s Haydn's op.

54,1 Quartet seemed
all-the-more

a unity of
satisfy

ing (though
always) re

fresh
ing intuit

ions.

Goethe

(and most es

pecially
Schiller'

s full–throat
ed drama

s) with e
ven less–than–

a–touch of
Shakespear

ian humour
ed down–spell

s.

Dialogue'

s more a

nearing–a
way from one'

s own prefer
ential self–

calling
s.

Sun-shine

happiness
es as if we'

ve been felt–
through with

flowering
color–imitat

ions.

April'

s sunshine

rained–in
alternat

ing self–den
ials.

Women'

s usually

more attent
ive dress–

finding per
sonings im

plies a self–
conscious

naked o
ver–aware

ness.

List-poem

s especial

ly those of
spring-flow

ers haven'
t yet learn

ed that each
flower breathe

s spaced-quiet
udes all-its-

own.

Writing

a poem with

someone more-
in-mind than

my own satis
fying that o

ther's need
for voice-ex

pressive
ness.

For Rosemarie'

s encompass

ing gladness
of her al

ways promis
ing smile.

Gottfried

Benn one of

the few who
calls word

s alive to
their other

wise sense
d-for-mean

ings.

Two-faced

Aren't we

all two-fac
ed The one

as of cloth
ed–appear

ances The o
ther masked

at a depth
of its un

knowing why
or wherea

bouts.

Charles Selig

er seeded his

surfaces with
unseen though

still–felt ap
pearance

s.

Charles Edward Ives (4)

a) historied

the song-depth
of an America

still inward
ly self-reveal

ing.

b) Hard to

keep one's

seat-downs
when Ives has

us clapping/
dancing his up

start folk-
songed reviv

als.

c) And those

lovely roman
tic vista

s landscap
ing his own

beautified
source-for-

place.

d) Ives

the spirit

of an Ameri
ca's (as

then) unlost
pristine

open-voice
d.

Has the

South still

seceeded
from an A

merica of
its lesser-

choice.

Heritage

Those book

s rowed on
my many shel

ve's an out-
touched heri

tage of al
ways no-re

turns.

He lay dy

 ing in a

 world of
 early spring'

 s refresh
 ing green

 ness as if
 it could col

 or him fully–
 through its

 life–encom
 passing

 s.

A symphon

ic concert

of Haydn Mo
zart and Beet

hoven with
Haydn's last

symphony
at the end

of its very-
beginning'

s continu
ous alive as

the finality
of a father'

s on-and-off
reclaiming

siblings.

If (as

he claimed)

the German
s will al

ways resent
the Jews for

having-been-
killed-off

at their own
hand's Lady

Macbeth-like
that blood

seeping in
to the very-

depths of
their alway

s blemish
ed time-be

ing.

The way

that blood-

gifted sur-
geon slowly

assumed the
transpar

ent fine
ness-flow of

his hand-glov
ed appreciat

ing readi
ness.

Janáček'

s natural

rough-har
monic expos

ures peasant
ly earthed–

down.

Strangely-e

nough it was

only "The Law"
(Torah) dead–

down graded
by St. Paul

that kept the
Jewish people

(God's first
beloved)

spiritual
ly alive o

ver two millen
iums of Christ

ian self-super
iority.

Beethoven'

s 4th piano

concerto rhy
thmically

dialogued
its urging

need for a
question

ed-respon
se.

"You can at

least write-it–
off" as if the

cleansing use–
of-words could

protect us
against those

so pre–estab
lished inter

ior darkness
es.

Earth-depthed (5)

a) *Why bury*

your gold

safely un
known to all

but yourself
if they'll

take the
blood-length

out of your
earth-depth

ed remain
s.

b) *Squirrel*

s bury their

nuts but u
sually for

get to find
them while

branch-swing
ing a seem

ingly higher
acrobatic

cause.

c) Too late

(as with Judas)

he realized
the all-con

suming depth
of a no-way

s-back.

d) My father

once said to

me "bury
your mistake

s" as if the
earth could

hold such an
untold depth

of my self-
forgotten

wounds.

e) At the end

of the war

They buried
their death–

shot Jews
washed–back

to the sur
face of their

unreconcil
ing guilt.

As one

thought

leads to a
nother as a

ladder hold
ing–fast to

one's stepp
ed–wise un

certain
ties.

Vaguely-mut

ed leaves
shadow

ing the sur
face of an

indecipher
able cause.

When really

in-need Help

often come
s from an un

expected per
son One

you wouldn'
t have want

ed to help-
out whatever

cause of his-
own.

To the death

of a Grecian
street-dog

who didn't
bark or wres

tle with teeth
ed-boned re

mains They
simply closed

their shut
ers down on

their unre
vealing sad

nesses.

Those first

gardened flow

ering-exposure
s cut-down

as a new-
born baby de

prived of
its living

breath.

A fine

ly design

ed bouquet-
of-flower

s at just-the-
right close

ly-express
ed oneness

as a staged-
on antipode

to Beethoven'
s emotion

al over-reach.

As she new

ly turned
boy-becoming

(once again)
the she of

a gender-mix
unbodied un

revealing
identity.

El Greco

elongat

ing his al
most bodi

less figure
s to a lyri

cally self-in
habiting o

therness-
finds.

Cézanne'

s small mount

ain oft climb
ing his paint-

and-easel to
a newly-

height of
self-return

s.

Piano Sonata *(D 894 Schubert) (3)*

a) 1ˢᵗ movt.

Those close

ly-kept
thoughts

however se
cretly in

triguing
at first as

the fabric
of a newly

worn dress
fades with the

more of its
repeated wear

ings.

b) The beauty

of life be

comes the
more–so of

it's losing
grasp on

us.

c) The danced-

likeness

of life slow
ly evolving

into the
finality of

a dance-of-
death.

Still leave

s the quiet

ing shadow
s of late

afternoon'
s oncoming

darkness
es.

Book-appearances

How often

have we read
ourselve

s into the
book-appear

ances of an
other with

out really
haven't

changed at–
all.

Blow-fished

He became

so unaware
of his own

self-import
ance as a

blow-fish
simulating

the bigness
of a lesser–

catch.

Blossom

ing trees

coloring
the shadow

s within the
unknown depth

of his self–
encompass

ings.

Hermelin

the pianist

eased himself
into the

light–rhy
thmic–efficien

ces of Haydn'
s sonata in a

minor key (e

minor) almost
thorough

ly hidden from
its presumed

sadness–e
voking call

ings.

Brahms'

early (op. 5)

sonata at
times rough–ed

ged with a
youthful self–

indulging
passion (but

then) cleared–
down to an in

timacy of
scarcely o

verheard si
lences.

Dürer'

s 1505 soft

ly modell
ed flesh-ton

ed Venetian
lady sensing-

us–through
Bellini-like

self-reassur
ances.

The ferris-

wheeled us

slowly over
hearing the

sky's spread
ing majestic

panorama
of its dark

ly prevail
ing light-im

pulsing
s.

Hermelin'

s Chopin-en

core moon-
lit entranc

ing an inti
mate world

secret
ly-sensed.

He couldn'

t "take-a-hint"

until word
lessly left-

alone (how
ever much he

tried) with a
one-sided

friendship.

Some are so

involved in

so many thing
s as busy-bee

's still sweet
ening from

their carous
ing after-ef

fects.

A. B.

realized

all other
s mirror

ing through
his own self-

apparent in
tention

s.

After his

   funeral

   she return
   ed to a

   house empt
   ied of all

   but her own
   self-enclos

   ing loneli
   ness.

He awoke

   in the midst
   of a night

   darkened
   with the dep

   th of his
   own self-shad

   owings.

Memory'

   s like a

   lost presen
   ce sunk in

   those ever-
   deepening

waters of a
once treas

ure-routed
ship.

Reborn

St. Paul

may have died
his old-per

son reborn to
much-the-same

life-pulse of
his alway

s-being.

Those far-

reaching

clouds drift
ing well be

yond his
thought-dis

solving in
terior accord

s.

Dialogue *(to the memory of Richard Crews)*

As he was

just–dead I
answered

back to his
55 years out–

of–my–life
(He couldn't

though he
would have cer

tainly liked
to) after 3 or

4 broken marr
iages ago he

must have re
mained self–

steadied to an
all–pursuing

goal which
when where.

Ray Poggenburg

He could

never "face–
up–to–him

self" hiding
his Jewish i

dentity from
his wife'

s most inti
mate touch

Even the mir
rors spoke-

back from a
hidden being

self-concious
ly otherwise.

It rain

ed over

night the
trees awak

ened from
their sound

lessly a
live presen

ce.

That

seldom-re

fining touch
of these

tiny self-im
plying flower

ings.

For Rosemarie

He often

realized
the poem bett

er–recalled
through

your self-
mirror

ing expos
ures.

These arter

ial branch–

routing
tree's rhy

thmic recall
ings.

Sensed-being

Does the think

ing again of
dead-person

s alive them
to a shadow

ing other
wise sensed–

being.

Open-wound

ed sap runn

ing the tree
down his

dried-from
instinct

ual presen
ce.

Though

fully-armour

ed with his
medieval

up-right
eous sword

Pink could
only imagine

his perilous
horse quixot

ically time-
charging.

When the

bird stopp

ed circling
the sky in

to the revol
ving depth

of its sha
dowing

momen
tarily still

nesses.

Dead-end

as if what

had always
been simply

stopped a no
wheres be

yond his own
sense-of-be

ing.

Mowing the

> first innocent
>
> ly self-find
> ing flowers
>
> The grass
> now sweetly
>
> scented
> with death'
>
> s all-consum
> ing after
>
> touch.

Weekend in that

to-and-from train-ensuing

Ludwigsburg (26)

> *a) This pre-summ*
>
> er greenness
>
> so lush as if
> his eyes o
>
> pening the
> grasses' color
>
> ing depth
> s.

b) *Accordion*

mood–music
the sadness

of dance
moon–enchant

ing its dis
tantly touch–

felt water
s.

c) *An unwritten*

day unremem
bered as if

words could
replace those

fading sound–
felt image

s.

d) *Ludwigsburg*

a city castle

ed in aristo
cratic ob

livion of its
unreclaim

ing past.

e) These morn

ing curtain
s the only

fineness-
touch of a

room larger
than its win

dowed light–ap
pearance

could inward
ly reveal.

f) A friend

ship restor
ed as a

landscape
increas

ingly self–re
defining.

g) A face

less woman
only remem

bered through
a brooch

strung to an
eyed–touch

truly–natur
al semi–pre

cious.

h) A city-

rain deep
ly brood

ing its un
reclaim

ing shadow
ing–light.

i) It could

only recall

a slight–
shift of

meaning as
clouds re

telling the
birth of a

single mo
ment.

j) For Rosemarie

Love is be

cause what
I sense and

the way you
are seemed

so inexpli
citly you.

k) That so-

called "per
sonal touch"

left him im
personal

ly artifi
cially un

touched from
such unduly

self-expos
ing appear

ances.

l) Against Freud

Man has learn

ed to wear
various

ly colored
clothes to

protect him
from his na

kedly self-re
vealing in

stinct
s.

m) "How much

poetry can
one read"

is like ask
ing how much

life is worth
seeing.

n) Rained-

down city

washed–clean
of its other

wise artifi
cially-faced

shadowing
s.

o) Roomed to

a quiet in
timacy of cur

tained–touch
ed felt-

through mo
ment

s.

p) Ludwigsburg

three-castl

ed city of arti
ficially plann

ed spacious
ly French-imi

tating cultur
ed garden

s.

q) 1. Conference

A rare "ar

chaic" medi
cal profess

or romanti
cally wash

ed-through
with melodic

over-flow
s.

r) 2. A clown

red-facing

us in-to con
gestions

of hysteri
cal bouts

of imitat
ing laught

er.

s) 3. A paunchy

middle-aged

cabaret
ist indecent

ly time-fac
ing us with

illusion
s of a self–

saving past.

t) Red curtain

s closing–
down on an o

therwise
colorless

ly self-emana
ting city's

blandly adapt
ing view.

u) Swabian Alb

These flow
ing-down

hills never
theless as

suming a
posture of

a teacher
flexibly

self–assert
ing.

v) What once
bred "evil
flowers" here

now harmless
ly attend

ing fluent
fields of un

informly color
ing brightly

indigenous
weeds.

w) She made a
freshly–
dressed self–

confident
impression

though with
attitud

ing side–
view mir

rors.

x) She became

so earnest
ly ready to

defend as a
perpetual

ly undersiz
ed goal-keep

er.

γ) Train-stat

ioned to a
windowed

self–assum
ing scholar

ly pose.

Rain-down

colors wash

ed away in
to streams

of lost–time
reflection

s.

His father

dying into
those soft-

waves of Gab
riel Fauré'

s "In Para
dise" death-

masked.

The juggler

dressed-in

off-set color
ings between

those weight
less realm

s of air-a
bandoning

space-find
s.

Winter-

gardens air-

spaced as
if glass could

fully encom
pass that

light–sens
ing outsided

ness.

The clown

(2nd cousin
to Shakes

peare's

fool)–play
ed neverthe

less on our
interior-

safety clos
ed–off inhab

itings.

That every-

recurring

tiny–color
ed bird

branch–sway
ing as a

child's swing
ing high for

sky–reach.

He awoke in

to a strange

ly otherwis
ed room dark

ened from all
remember

ed home–call
ings.

"We're all

in it togeth

er" as if
life had be

come its own
time–complet

ing labyrin
th.

He never

could forget
that strange

ly evocat
ive house-of–

clocks each
timed to a

differing
start–route

but now all–
together

stopped to a
timeless

void.

She felt as

if she'd never

fully grown–up
to her father'

s towering image.

Virgin'

s not-so-
much what's

happened
or-not But

more that in
nocently

naïve child-
like way of

lifing it
through safe

ly light-mu
ted color

ings.

The multi-

colored rain

bow spanning
The Lord's

heavenly re
sponse even to

a world drown
ed in its e

ver-recurr
ing waves of

self-indulg
ence.

F minor piano Quintet *(Brahms slow mvt.)*

a continu

ous dialogue
as if the

real scope
of slow mvts.

wasn't to
be found as

a well to
its depthed–

in founda
tions.

Piano Quintet *(Brahms)*

so dramatic

ally colored
as if Beet

hoven (as
Schumann tru

ly believed)
reappear

ing in a new
romantic

guise.

Tchaikov

sky's 1st Quar
tet so folk-

attuned sim
ply repeat

ing variat
ions temper

ed to an al
most atypical

phrased-
through un

ity-of-sound.

Haven't

each-of-us
been called

to create
our own ark

on this dry-
land of wash-

out faith-
routes.

Biblical "persons" *(8)*

a) Cain in pre-

Voltairean

manner culti
vating his

own garden
ed–delight

s at-the-
cost-of real

izing its al
ways–source

and master.

b) David

(as the Heb
rews at Jeri

cho) walled–
out from his

own self–satis
fying death–

urge.

c) Saul mirror

ing his peo

ple's king
ly desires

for a "pagan"
ruler fell–

victim to
that cave's

interior dark
ness of his

own no–longer
faith–inhabi

ting solitary-
self.

d) Peter

that alway
s–fisher

man netted
at his–own

lake's call
ing nothing

but lost–hope
s and the

need for a
nother's

voiced–guid
ance.

e) Thomas

so realisti
cally self-

attuned that
his-own fin

gered-disbe
liet touched-

in-to the
bloodless

scars of Jesus'
bodied resurr

ecting-self.

f) Zacchaeus'

proverbial
smallness

still adept
at climbing

to-the-top
of his own

eagerness-
calling

s.

g) Mordechai

that never-re
linguish

ing voice of
Israel's God–

chosen call
ings beauti

fied Esther e
ven-more

with the spir
itual depth

of her God-
given appeal

s.

h) Jesus him

self writt
en-through

his own E
mancipat

ing Declara
tion from the

slavery of
our self-deter

mining in
habiting

self.

Thereabout

She always
s wanted to

be what she
always wasn'

t – Some child
ren like to

feel themsel
ves into o

ther names
But she want

ed to change
her entire be

ing an
unknown but

always remain
ing therea

bouts.

Her house *(for Lenore)*

a picture–
book illustrat

ing the phase
s of her hus

band's spirit
ual–artist

ic growth un
til the paint

ers took those
pictures down

left her (some
how) nakedly

alone.

Punctuating

as if those
very-moment

s held-in
camera-near

could be pun
ctuated to a

live-stop.

Sound-sense

Those ambigu
ities of

language
d-meaning

may be decept
ively lead

ing us down
nameless

corridor
s of unequal

led sound-
sense.

He always

remained so
pre-occupied

as a sound–
proof wall

one couldn'
t penetrate

beyond its
stone-like

self-assum
ing appear

ance.

This sweet

ening scent
of lilac's so

richly self–
fulfilling

dreams even
of moon-en

chanting
celestial

garden
s.

This summer

greened in
to a satiat

ed self–sat
isfying full

ness.

Explain

ing a poem'
s like

T. S. Eliot'
s kind–of–

footnotes
bottoming

whatever'
s said should

have been
self–reali

zing.

Listen

ing to the
rain's soft

appeals as
as woman

fleshed to
touched–await

ings.

He could no

longer keep-
up with him

self like
running a

race beyond
a phantom-

shadowed be
ing.

Dark

rains in
habiting e

ver-deeper
those omin

ous self-sha
dowing

s.

If there'

s no word
for it's

still oppres
sing these

wordless
silence

s.

For Rosemarie

You've har

boured this
wandering

Jew of my
restless

ly anchor
ed deeper-

down
s.

If we'

re still
holding-back

that little
dog's long

ing-for-life
We may be

come (in
time) leashed

to our own
short-line

fears.

If each of

Haydn's 107 sym
phonies mir

rors a world
separate and

uniquely with
in itself Why

can't these
numerous poem

s reflect each-
its-own-moment

s of a contin
uously self-

evolving al
ways-now.

This self-

enclosing
intimate

ly seclus
ive tulip-

world open
ing only to

its dried-
down death-ap

peals.

Calling-the shots

The caddy

helped call
ing-the-shot

s as if his
distanc

ing eye-length
s could re

veal the
swing of his

"master's" ball-
down settling-

control.

For Warren

Sometime

s the acute
critic can

realize
more of the

poet's in
stinctive

word-sense.

Is a preach

er there to

measure the
appeal to his

life–like aud
ience down

far–below Or
should he be

standing
high–above to

God's ever–de
manding word–

claims–on–
us.

Contrasts

Van Gogh may

have painted
even–before

realizing
why Whereas

Gauguin need
ed to be

landscap
ed into

the express
ive color

s of his
own tenta

ive response.

El Greco'

s ecstati

cally holy-
spirited out

pouring fig
urations

disembod
ied my own in

timate quiet
udes of pray

er–sense.

Charles

left behind
so many year

s-of-paint
ings that

walled her in
to his pre–

designing
touched–in

tuition
s.

Creation of Adam (Michelangelo)

At the cen

ter that fin
ger-touch

life-creat
ing man's

realiz
ing his

God-given
self.

Big talker

s often need
the more-of–

silence to
help replent

ish their
breath-forsak

en shadow
ing-self.

Rosemarie'

s softening
modestly re

fining appear
ance continu

es to hold
my shadow

ing-unease
there if no–

wheres–else.

An art that

tells all it
has to say

fails to ig
nite that

somewhere
s within

leaving litt
le space for

our self-ex
ploring re

sponse.

Are those

who seem hard
ly changed

after year
s apart still

more–of–them
selves than

those who ap
pear strange

ly differ
ent.

That "unanswered question"

(after Charles Edward Ives)

spaces its
own response

if only by e
choing

the very-
depth of our

personed-be
ing.

Schubert'

s "unfinish
ed symphony"

completed it
self as a bro

ken-off con
versation

because of
their noth

ing more's to-
be-said.

If we hard

ly ever "live-

through-our-
children"

(then perhaps)
it's only the

name that fu
tures us be

yond the
grave's in

delibly in
scribed fin

alized de
cision.

Lilies-of-the-valley'

s tiny bell-
white moment

s intricate
ly lined to

a process
ional of al

most unheard
gentle-sound

ings.

For Rosemarie

whose indwell
ing light

ens the sun
less depth

of these
rain–bespok

en spring–
time day

s.

Joseph Martin

Kraus' newly
discovered

Concerto for
Viola and

Cello dis
lodging a

depthed–flow
continuous

ly self–re
vealing.

"The rest is silence" (Shakespeare)

still e
choing that

painful loss
of nothing

left-to-say.

For Mother at age 104

Her generat
ion may have

all died-out
each with that

unspoken loss
of her left–

alone with
the failing

songs of her
youth and

that faint
ly twilight

atmosphere
of once-hav

ing-been.

Dad

as an astute
lawyer saw

through
those oft

self-sooth
ing decept

ive poses of
others But be

ing a dream
er himself

built his own
castles in the

sand–flowing
waves of time'

s overcom
ing reach.

Each familiar

gravestone
seems yet a

live retell
ing what's now

become invis
ibly heard.

If "it

couldn't be
better said"

A sound-proof
for good poet

ry as a cam
era's recall

ing look in
sistent

ly there.

Home (for Rosemarie)

has become
for me not

a place but
a personed-

together
ness And if

she should
die home

would become
as a house

homeless
ly vacant.

At the airport

Crowds of

stone-shad
ows scarce

ly illumina
ting the shall

ow depths of
these always–

present arti
ficial light

s.

Cloud-

view as gath

ering thought
s distant

ly self-involv
ing.

Pink

well-suited

to the present
tight-fitting

mode smiling
itself through

those color
ing rapture

s of button
ed–up self–

presentat
ion.

The baby

with the plead
ing eyes

asking more
than she could

realize why.

Clarinet Sonata (Weinberg)

A space-lone

ly voice re
trieving a

loss that
touched some
where at the

center of his
time-griev

ing self.

Erna'

s down-stair
ed high-light

ing hand-felt
sculpture

s left Ernest
with his dee

per-sculpted
eyes unstair

ed to his
only provis

ional pre-
sence.

Touching

artificial

flowers so
dryly color-

sensed that
his hands

seemed al
most blood

lessly un
real.

Elisabeth

could only

read the emp
ty sylla

bles of a
German lang

uage dead
(for her) to

its "innate"
callings for

Jewish blood.

The high-

German of

Vienna's rich
ly-endow

ed Jewish comm
unity then low

ered to the
feared–gutt

ers of a
speechless

death-route.

For most

    of the few

    remaining
    Jews-of-Vienna

    became a no-re
    turning to

    those aband
    oned coffee

    houses and the
    nostalgic

    culture made-
    more in

    their own i
    mage of a ghost

    ly inhabit
    ing past.

The flag'

    s no longer

    "high-fly
    ing" but sol

    emnly red-
    striping the

    blood-line
    s of its fail

    ing world-do
    minance.

Why flower

s even bloom
in bad time

s celebrat
ing a contin

uous life-im
pulsing

beauty.

Sandy

her face

blunted now
almost harsh

ly self-escap
ing wound

s that time
had cancell

ed-out her
once so self-

convincing
mannered-

stance.

The night

mysterious

ly moon–a
wake The tree

s as if call
ed to the

height of
their long–

impending
searching

silence
s.

Ways of Nature *(17, Seliger 2008)*

Growth–si

lences color
ing the seed

s of nature'
s spacial

ly interior–
designs.

My sister

Doris' aging

face perpetua
ting a death-

masked unan
swering quest

ions.

Self-praise

blow-fished

beyond the e
ver-scratch

ing surface
of his all-

inflating
self-image.

Rebecca'

s self-assum
ing dressed

in a display
of command

ing color-
designing

her richly
decorated

African heri
tage.

Cowan'

s once–a–year
waiting for

no–one–o
ther than ...

croaching
as an aware

ness–lion
ready to

pounce upon
my very–near

ing appear
ance.

Village-of-

Scarsdale
windowing

as a giant
telescope

unseen world
s of blue–

timed space
lessness.

What will

that little
two-year-old

Emma with
the window-o

pen eyes re
member once

she's forgott
en all that

a two-year-
old child can'

t remember
at all.

The sound

s of the sea
distantly e

choing
through the

sand–surfa
ces of these

thought-felt
moments.

For Rosemarie I

I could still-

feel your soft
ening eyes

touch-awaken
ing the very-

depth of these
timeless dark

nesses.

For Rosemarie II

Sometime
s these much-

used paths
realizing

the very-
length of our

timed-togeth
erness.

For Neil

when blue be

comes the
tree-feeling

of its sky-o
pening one

ness-beyond.

These left-

over paint

ings housed
us in room

s disturb
ingly off–

center
ed.

Dementia

She stared
through me

as if I
wasn't real

ly there
owl–like

treed to her
avidly branch

ed–confine
ments.

A piano

rarely used
though still–

echoing
those long–

forgotten
finger's

self-reveal
ing.

For N. R.'

s room with

its lush gar
dened–view

as if green
had become

the focus of
her own a

wakening si
lences.

Immanuel

Kant never left
his native

Königsberg
bombed-out

renamed re
built an ugly

imperson
al style with

only a statue
of him star

ing through
the time–space

of its last
German re

mains.

Free-fly

ing birds
at the upp

er reaches
of this town'

s soulless
ly self–in

habiting sha
dows.

Can bare-

touched stone
s be seen

as the dead
archives

of time's un
remember

ed past.

She I

forever chatt
ering the

limbed-full
ness of her

usual imitat
ing monkey-

tree.

She II

once a quite
delicious

ly alluring
nymph now

matronly as
suming a

position
of somewhat

challeng
ing social

virtues.

Teddy-eye

acting-out
all of his

potential
theatrical-

parts with
still cyclop

tic intent
ions.

If life' *(for Warren)*

s the true
theme of all

these "minor"
little poem

s (then) e
ven the tin

iest of flow
ers breaking

through the
pavement'

s stepped-
down inertia

deserves the
creative puls

ings of these
poetic-say

s.

Why opera'

s not-my-thing
(ever tempt

ing eyes and
sounds) too

dressed-up in
the musical

clothes of
its less-effi

cient dramat
ic art.

For Ingo and

Solvey anchor

ed to an o
therwise

past than my
own now sam

ed to our
pre-ordain

ed future-
felt time-

claims.

Twilight-

times when

a world of
light shadow

ed into
vague inbe

coming mut
ed silence

s.

Romance *(Piano Concerto 20, Mozart)*

a child-like

purity of
soundless

ly recalling
those most in

timate of
self-reflect

ions.

Mozart's *(no. 21 k. 467)*

C Major Piano
concerto all

so classical
ly-bright

seldom heard
in the 19th

centurie's
obsession

with tragical
ly unrelent

ing darkness
es.

Piano Concerto 9 *(Mozart, k. 271 slow mvt.)*

a world so

suddenly
newly creat

ed out of
inner sadness

es unspoken
in a world of

fashion
able over

sights.

Do Mozart' *(N. R.)*

s finales

seem in-any-
way superfi

cially engag
ing Brilliant

but that dark
er sense-e

vading.

For Chung

after the

death-of-his-
wife simply

disappear
ed the way

widows once
(in India)

threw them
selves upon

the burning
pyre His that

burned-out
guilty-sense

of self-immol
ation.

Fragile

ly touched–a
wake tiny

flower
s dotted to

the why of
my own in

spoken eye-
sense.

For Rosemarie

How you will

read these
words–alive

only because
they've been

completed
through the

silence
s of your

self-contem
plative sens

ings.

It seemed

to him as

if that train
had missed

its in–betw
een stop

ped only at
the end of

his very-be
ings.

The Hellen

ic birth of
the dark seed

s of tragedy
parallell

ed a sculp
ture of A

pollonic
beauty void

of all inter
ior shadow

ings.

The fear

of no-more-
you A vacan

cy at the
very-center

of self A
loss of why

life and
love have be

come so in
creasing

ly samed.

Illmensee

soft-waved
a self-con

fining world
enclosed in

its own sense-
of-being.

Mobbed

One really

doesn't know
the why or

wherefore
They cut her

off from
their self-en

circling self
to that hurt–

loneliness
at an age of

needing-for-
more.

Some compos

ers create
d more for

the idiomat
ic accord

s of their
self-intun

ing voice
Chopin piano

ed its black
and white sha

dowings
while Mendels

sohn voiced
a natural

leisure of
choired ex

pressive
ness.

This sumptu

ous month of
May flower

ed me in
its dense

ly color
ing garden

of such rapt
urous scent

s that I be
came perfum

ed to a no–
way–wish for

getting–out.

She seemed

as a juicy
fruit-tree

fleshed–out
of much of

its tempting
sap–runn

ing phase
s.

Seems

It seems

that minist
ers should

become as
sexless as

their wooden
ed–empty

pewed–out
sermon

s.

The Cherry Orchard *(Chekhov) (3)*

a) When per

sons become
more than

their reali
zing self

Timed to a
place–defin

ing change.

b) The Cherry

Orchard person

alized its own
claims on their

life–death
sequencing

s.

c) Chekhov'

s time of
class–change

of rising
capital

ism (a near
foil to Budden

brooks) couldn'
t fully real

ize the length
of Russia's

new–becoming
s.

These new a

partment hou
ses all look

ing alike as
if pre-dat

ing the per
sons samed-

within.

If good

plays speak
in their own

terms Why over-
act them with

moderniz
ing song-and-

danced boister
ous routine

s.

It was the

way the sur
geon slow

ly but fine
ly attired

himself in
to his glov

ed–smooth
ness as if

the blood–
signs could

(therewith)
be faintly

self–distan
cing.

"No animal

s allowed"
an old–age

home inhab
iting noth

ing more
than loss the

loneliness
of not e

ven a pet to
warm–up their

own self-pro
tective in

stinct
s.

Whitsun I

the birth-
hour of The

Church or of
each burn

ing with a
faith preach

ed to their
own intim

ate-being
worded just–

for-them.

Whitsun II

a leafed-
mosaic wind–

spreading
of the word

birthed in
the spirit

of a recept
ive-oneness.

Israel

ghetto

ed again
st all those

restless
tides reestab

lishing its
biblical God–

plan.

Peonese

densely
as if snow–

intact form
ed-enclosure

's only es
cape routes

to a bloss
oming full

ness.

Helpless

ly raped in
to the with

holding dark
ness of her

feared and
worldless si

lence
s.

Some wound

s (as those
cancer-plagu

ed) repeat
edly opening

out their
blood–clean

sing need
s.

Sistine Madonna *(Raphael, Dresden)*

Not even the

newly golden–
framed Sistine

Madonna could
convince me

of more than
its posed

(sentimental
ly angell

ed as well)
perfectly bal

anced-being.

Largo

(Jean Baptiste Barrière, Sonata 2, Book 2)

> a simplici
>
> ty of a two-
> voiced one
>
> ness space-
> timing.

Adagio *(Barrière, Sonata 2, Book 4)*

(for Ingo and Solvey)

> The broad
> ly depthed–
>
> length of
> the cello's
>
> sustain
> ing glow.

He died

> what we
> could be
>
> thinking
> together
>
> now those
> untold dark
>
> nesses bet
> ween.

"Judaeo-Christian"

as if we
could reshape

what real
ly should have

been by call
ing it other

wise than
its truly

Grecian
source

realized.

Still life

s can still
us to those

cool space
s touch-in

habiting
the colors

of their
self-refin

ing near
ness.

Crossword *(for Manfred and Carol)*

puzzles per
haps intend

ed as a mapp
ed–plan of

our blacked–
in space

s myster
iously non–

being.

Computer

virus–war

s attacking
the very

blood–stream
s of man'

s non–be
ing.

When her hus

band died
their glass

ed out–look
ing window

ed–house
keep clos

ing in u
pon her seld

omed alone
lines.

The nearer

to the stage
the more of

one's close-
up almost

actively in
volved appear

ances.

Why after

The Rite of
Spring did

Stravinsky
pre-cooled him

self down
(perhaps in

fear of his
own excess

es) neo-class
ically.

Though Ibsen *(for Donna)*

repeated
those same

themes over–
and–again

each time
as if fresh

ly first–
heard.

He decision

ed his life
so adamant

ly self–as
sured that e

ven his mirr
ored–look

ing back at
what he had

n't become
anymore.

Some

thing was
missing He

knew but
couldn't find-

where in a
house of self-

deceptive
back-stair

ed passage
s.

Poetry books by David Jaffin

1. **Conformed to Stone,** Abelard-Schuman, New York 1968, London 1970.

2. **Emptied Spaces,** with an illustration by Jacques Lipschitz, Abelard–Schuman, London 1972.

3. **In the Glass of Winter,** Abelard-Schuman, London 1975, with an illustration by Mordechai Ardon.

4. **As One,** The Elizabeth Press, New Rochelle, N. Y. 1975.

5. **The Half of a Circle,** The Elizabeth Press, New Rochelle, N. Y. 1977.

6. **Space of,** The Elizabeth Press, New Rochelle, N. Y. 1978.

7. **Preceptions,** The Elizabeth Press, New Rochelle, N. Y. 1979.

8. **For the Finger's Want of Sound,** Shearsman Plymouth, England 1982.

9. **The Density for Color,** Shearsman Plymouth, England 1982.

10. **Selected Poems** with an illustration by Mordechai Ardon, English/Hebrew, Massada Publishers, Givatyim, Israel 1982.

11. **The Telling of Time,** Shearsman, Kentisbeare, England 2000 and Johannis, Lahr, Germany.

12. **That Sense for Meaning,** Shearsman, Kentisbeare, England 2001 and Johannis, Lahr, Germany.

13. **Into the timeless Deep,** Shearsman, Kentisbeare, England 2003 and Johannis, Lahr, Germany.

14. **A Birth in Seeing,** Shearsman, Exeter, England 2003 and Johannis, Lahr, Germany.

15. **Through Lost Silences,** Shearsman, Exeter, England 2003 and Johannis, Lahr, Germany.

16. **A voiced Awakening,** Shearsman, Exter, England 2004 and Johannis, Lahr, Germany.

17. **These Time-Shifting Thoughts**, Shearsman, Exeter, England 2005 and Johannis, Lahr, Germany.

18. **Intimacies of Sound,** Shearsman, Exeter, England 2005 and Johannis, Lahr, Germany.

19. **Dream Flow** with an illustration by Charles Seliger, Shearsman, Exeter, England 2006 and Johannis, Lahr, Germany.

20. **Sunstreams** with an illustration by Charles Seliger, Shearsman, Exeter, England 2007 and Johannis, Lahr, Germany.

21. **Thought Colors,** with an illustration by Charles Seliger, Shearsman, Exeter, England 2008 and Johannis, Lahr, Germany.

22. **Eye-Sensing,** Ahadada, Tokyo, Japan and Toronto, Canada 2008.

23. **Wind-phrasings,** with an illustration by Charles Seliger, Shearsman, Exeter, England 2009 and Johannis, Lahr, Germany.

24. **Time shadows,** with an illustration by Charles Seliger, Shearsman, Exeter, England 2009 and Johannis, Lahr, Germany.

25. **A World mapped-out,** with an illustration by Charles Seliger, Shearman, Exeter, England 2010.

26. **Light Paths,** with an illustration by Charles Seliger, Shearsman, Exeter, England 2011 and Edition Wortschatz, Schwarzenfeld, Germany.

27. **Always Now,** with an illustration by Charles Seliger, Shearsman, Bristol, England 2012 and Edition Wortschatz, Schwarzenfeld, Germany.

28. **Labyrinthed,** with an illustration by Charles Seliger, Shearsman, Bristol, England 2012 and Edition Wortschatz, Schwarzenfeld, Germany.

29. **On the Other Side of Self,** with an illustration by Charles Seliger, Shearsman, Bristol, England 2012 and Edition Wortschatz, Schwarzenfeld, Germany.

Book on David Jaffin's poetry: Warren Fulton, **Poemed on a beach,** Ahadada, Tokyo, Japan and Toronto, Canada 2010.